SMOKE TRAILS IN THE SKY

P/O A.C. BARTLEY. D.F.C.   92 (FIGHTER) SQUADRON.

S/Ldr A C Bartley,
DFC & bar by Cuthbert Orde

SMOKE TRAILS IN THE SKY

TONY BARTLEY, DFC & bar

Crécy

SMOKE TRAILS IN THE SKY

This revised new edition published in 1997 by
Crécy Publishing Limited

First published in 1984 by William Kimber & Co. Ltd

ISBN 0 947554 63 7

Printed and bound in Great Britain by
Biddles Ltd, Guildford and King's Lynn

Crécy Publishing Limited
Southside, Manchester Airport,
Wilmslow, Cheshire. SK9 4LL

CONTENTS

Preface

According to King's Regulations and Air Council's Instructions (para 786), a pilot was required to keep a Pilot's Flying Log Book. The instructions were as follows: (1) This book is an official document and is the property of His Majesty's Government; (2) An accurate and detailed record is to be kept in the log of all flights undertaken by the individual to whom it relates.

These records kept by rule have been augmented by my diaries, letters written to my parents and present-day recollections of my own, together with those of some of my friends with whom I served in the war.

AB

Acknowledgements

My warmest thanks to the people who have helped me in the writing of this book: old comrades-in-arms Brian Kingcome, 'Tich' Havercroft, Al Wright, Geoff Wellum, Don Kingaby, Harry Broadhurst and Jeff Quill.

CHAPTER ONE

Prelude to War

I liken life to a game of cricket. A challenge to defend oneself against a relentless foe, ever watching and waiting for the mistake which ends one's innings. At a score of fifty, one raises one's bat to the applause of the crowd, and thanks God for his mercies. From then on, the game is not of paramount importance, since one has achieved, at least, a substance of success to have survived as long. One knows that the bowling will eventually prevail.

I started my innings in Judge's House, Ramna, Dacca, Bengal, India where I was born. My father was the District Judge which he had never intended. He was born an Irishman, became a scholar and all he wanted out of life was a Fellowship of his college, Trinity Dublin, which he missed on account of his inability to complete his final exams due to a severe case of tonsillitis. So he had to seek an alternative career, and, with a double first and Vice Chancellor's medals for Greek and Latin, he was welcomed by the Indian Civil Service and entered their colonial establishment at the age of twenty-four.

There, he met my mother, Marjorie Hamilton, whose father had been a partner in an East India Company. The Hamiltons were big operators in the British Raj. They married, and thereafter my mother determined to procreate a family, between her predilections to playing bridge, golf, tennis and shooting tigers. My sister, myself and brother were born within the next four years and in the fifth, taken to England where my brother and I were deposited in a kindergarten, my sister in a girls' school nearby, our mother returning to India.

As life progressed, my brother and I were enrolled on another parental visit in a preparatory school, the headmaster of which, we were to experience to our terror, maintained discipline by a public beating of the transgressor. We had made up our minds to run away, but not where to, when our mother reappeared fortuitously from India, and on becoming aware of our intentions, enrolled us in another prep school.

This headmaster had two pretty daughters, and agreed to

accommodate further our sister who had also premeditated a bolt from her establishment. We enjoyed this new set-up, were treated with affection, and decided we would make the school our home. When our parents visited us, periodically, we holidayed in hotels in Eastbourne. I found it hard to recognise my father.

When I had reached fourteen years of age, my mother decided that the family should have a home of their own, primarily on account of the late addition of my second sister, a planned procreation to celebrate my father's elevation to the High Court of Calcutta. She was dubbed the High Court baby. Parental commuting had, by then, been facilitated by international air transport and by my father's salary increment. This home was located in Buckinghamshire, in the proximity of Stowe School, where I was to conclude my secondary education.

Unlike my father, I was completely uninterested in academic achievements, and devoted my time to sport in which I achieved a pretty good all-round reputation as an athlete. During my last year at school, I decided that I was only wasting my parents' money, and that I'd better get going with the career that had been parentally prepared: to join an East India company with family connections. This required an apprenticeship to a firm of Chartered Accountants in London which was the most soul-destroying experience I can remember, and after twelve months I quit, threw away my 'bowler' and went down to Blackheath Rugby Football Club where I had played with their captain, Gus Walker, an air force officer whom I greatly admired.

Gus was one of those who thought that Hitler was intent on war, and one evening after a game and over a pint of beer, suggested that if I didn't want to join the Territorials, how about the RAF?

Having given this a lot of thought, I determined to try the air for size, and got my mother's blessing and financial support to join the West Malling Flying Club in Kent. After eight hours of dual instruction on Tiger Moths, I went solo, and got hooked on flying. This was late 1938.

However, before the Rubicon was crossed, I decided to visit Germany and see what was going on for myself. In Frankfurt-on-Main, I house-guested with acquaintances of my parents they had met on one of their travels.

One day, on an inspection of the magnificent botanical gardens, I met a middle-aged man who impressed me by his shaven head. On further acquaintance, I learned he was a distinguished Jew who had just been released from a concentration camp, his experiences in which he recounted, and invited me to his home to meet his family. When I related this experience to my hosts, they were horrified at my visit, and told me that either I terminate my new friendship, or return to England immediately. When I asked for a reason, I was told that their son, a Hitler Youth, would denounce his father to the Gestapo for harbouring a Jew fraterniser.

With that experience, and a conversation in a Frankfurt *Bierkeller* with two English-speaking bomber pilots who were keen to impress an Englishman with the might of their Luftwaffe, 'who could reduce London to rubble, but, of course there would be no need for that, as England would accept German terms, *Mein Herr*', I caught the ball Gus Walker had passed to me at Blackheath Rugby Football Club.

On my return from Germany, I told my mother of my feelings which had, in part, determined me to apply for a commission in the Royal Air Force as a pilot. She had also sensed the storm approaching maybe from correspondence with my hosts, hidden from their children, and didn't try to dissuade me.

May 1939 found me stationed at No 13 Flying Training School, Drem, Scotland, as an acting pilot officer on probation. A whole new life had opened up for me, and I knew that the next few months could make or break it. The sky was now my only goal, my only limit.

Besides recruiting pilots from the United Kingdom, the RAF had sought others from the British Commonwealth, and it has always been my belief that this diversity of nationalities formed the strength of the team that won the Battle of Britain. What one lacked, the other made up for, making the complementary force indestructible. However, with my family and school background and upbringing, I must confess that on first acquaintance with some of my commonwealth confederates, I thought some of them somewhat unhouse-trained.

I drove my open MG, with one suitcase in the back, from my preliminary school at Sywell in Northamptonshire, up to Scotland, and reported to the Station Adjutant, with my Movement Orders. Having noted my particulars, he assigned me my accommodation and told me, as soon as I had settled in, to report to the Chief Flying Instructor with my Flying Log Book.

Squadron Leader John Grandy (now Marshal of the Royal Air

Force and Governor of Windsor Castle), sitting at his desk, acknowledged my salute, took and flipped open my Log, studied my flying assessment from Sywell, then looked up and smiled:

'You'll do.'

It was somewhat of an anti-climax for me when I was assigned to twin-engined training, destined, at my graduation, to Bomber, Coastal or Transport Commands, and I used to watch with envy the soaring, looping, chasing and spinning single-engined Hawker Hart. The Airspeed Oxford, my training mount, was of wooden construction, slow, cumbersome and non-aerobatic. Just a sound work-horse for which it had been designed.

My day flying instructor, a Flight Lieutenant 'Scottie' Pryde, was a heavy-weight boxing champion, and had previously served in both the Foreign Legion and Fleet Air Arm. We soon became good friends. Jamie Rankin, who subsequently commanded 92 Fighter Squadron to which I belonged during the Battle of Britain at Biggin Hill, taught me my night flying.

In our off duty time, I learned to play golf, sail a thirty-two foot boat I'd bought with four of my friends and named Pimms No 4, went into Edinburgh with them on Saturday night drinking safaris, and fell madly in love with the Provost of Edinburgh's daughter.

When war was declared, just after I had got my Wings, I proved that the Oxford *was* acrobatic by looping the Firth of Forth Bridge, and nothing fell off.

In October 1939 I was posted to 92 Fighter Squadron at Tangmere, and after a gargantuan farewell party in the officers' mess, I headed my MG towards the south.

*

November 20th, 1939

On arrival at RAF Tangmere, the first thing I saw on passing through the Guard Room Gate was a circle of Blenheims dispersed around the airfield perimeter, and the sight made me shudder. After Drem, I had done a three-week conversion course at Hendon on this unreliable aircraft which had been converted into a night fighter for 92 Squadron to fly. If a motor cut on take-off, it could prove lethal in a restricted area such as Hendon, and the conversion course had suffered two fatal accidents, killing all on board.

I checked in with the Squadron Adjutant, and was assigned my billet in one of the married quarters which had been evacuated of marrieds. He told me that John Bryson, Harry Edwards and Howard Hill who had trained with me at Drem had just arrived from another conversion unit, which gave me some consolation. John and Harry were Canadians, Howard a New Zealander. I was then escorted to my new CO's office.

Roger Bushell was a South African and a bull of a man with a damaged eye from an accident with a ski pole which somehow didn't detract from his rugged attraction. Ten years older than I, he was a barrister by profession, who had learned most of his flying in the famous 601 Auxiliary Squadron. Its fame came through most of the members being either millionaires or sons thereof. Ninety-two had been formed by a few senior officers from this squadron under the command of Roger, or the Führer as we called him. His two flight commanders lounged in chairs, and I made a mental note of a handsome blond giant introduced as Paddy Green, also from South Africa who rose his six foot to greet me with a hand crusher, and a short squat character with an Irish brogue who didn't rise from his seat. Just grinned. Later, I got vibrations that Roger felt his second night commander was not in the league he was trying to build. He left the squadron when at Croydon was shot down and got himself repatriated from Stalag Luft POW camp.

Roger Bushell, Janie Montagu and Paddy Green at Cherkley

I met up with my Drem friends in the officers' mess, and they introduced me to three other new members of 92, graduates of the RAF College Cranwell – Bob Holland, Pat Learmond and Allan Wright. Bob was a gregarious drinking party man who played piano as good as I'd ever heard. Allan the antithesis: serious, religious, quiet. Pat, I had no time to get to know before I saw him die on the beach at Dunkirk, our first squadron casualty.

As six o'clock approached, we decided to meet up at the local pub which the boys had located to celebrate our good fortune in our new CO and one of our flight commanders, if not the other, and the dreaded aeroplane with which the squadron was to fly. Bob played piano until closing time, and Harry Edwards took over the bar while John Bryson went out to the car park with the bar maid, to look at the moon.

A new life line was starting for all of us. Few were to survive it.

*

With Howard Hill, Al, Bob and Pat Learmond

During the next few months, the 'phoney war' as this period became named, Roger Bushell trained his young squadron as a team: formation flying, night flying, searchlight co-operation, tactics and attack.

At the beginning of 1940, the squadron moved to Gatwick for a short spell, then settled at Croydon, a desperately inappropriate airfield for flying an unsuitable aircraft at night, due to its built-up surroundings. If a motor cut, you had had it, as was proved soon after, killing all on board. Notwithstanding, we accepted these hazards as par for the course and just longed to get into some action which had, so far, and fortuitously been denied us.

Then, on March 6th, three weeks before my twenty-first birthday, 92 Squadron was re-equipped with Spitfires. The bogey men of Blenheims and black nights had dawned into horizons of dawn sunlight's and blue skies.

One of the unique and most alarming experiences in one's life must surely be to find oneself alone in an aeroplane for the very first time, completely dependent upon oneself to get back to mother earth. In air terminology, this is called 'Soloing'. My second most exciting experience was to fly a Spitfire for the first time. It was like driving a racing car after an Austin…riding a racehorse, after a hack. It just didn't seem to want to slow down. When one pulled back the throttle, it took a long time to take effect on its speed.

In contrast to the Blenheim, the Spitfire was the perfection of a flying machine designed to combat and destroy its enemy. It had no vices, carried great fire power, and a Rolls Royce motor which very rarely stopped. An aerodynamic masterpiece, and a joy to fly.

The next weeks were spent in a hasty training programme as the inevitable confrontation with the Luftwaffe drew nearer. Front attack, stern attack, side attack, battle formation and air to ground firing. The first target I ever got the opportunity to shoot at in the air was a Me 109. The more proficient we became in mock combat, the more restless we were to get into the real thing, but our CO knew we were not yet qualified. We lacked a paramountly important element in our team – a second flight commander to replace the Irishman who had been posted to another squadron. He knew we were unprepared until he'd found one.

The arrival of Robert Stanford Tuck at Croydon was as spectacular as his reputation. He buzzed the airfield with every known and, to us, unknown acrobatic before making a perfect three point landing, and we watched in awe. We'd heard that he was an ace aerobatic pilot, crack shot, had once baled out in an aerobatic collision which had scarred his face, and been court martialled for beating up another airfield, but reprieved as some 'brass hat' knew that when the shooting started he would prove himself indispensable.

He lounged out of his cockpit, a silk scarf draped around his neck, a monogrammed handkerchief drooping from one sleeve. He lit a cigarette in a long white holder, and strolled towards our CO who had emerged on the dispersal area to greet him. We watched them pace the tarmac whilst in conversation, then exchange salutes, and Bob mount up his Spitfire and take off. Roger sauntered back to join his protégés, and grinning, told us that he had completed his team.

On May 7th the squadron moved to Northolt. Our training of our combat team had been completed, and all we wanted now was action.

The third week in May, a section of three led by Paddy Green, my

Bob Tuck

flight commander, escorted Churchill and his Chiefs of Staff in a Flamingo to and from Paris on a last resort mission to try and bolster French morale before their capitulation. I did not consider that there was any possibility of contact with the enemy, so, before leaving Le Bourget, I unloaded the ammunition from one of my machine gun tanks and substituted bottles of brandy. On landing back at Northolt, mission accomplished, my armourers, according to standard operational procedure, whipped open the ammunition bays to check re-armament, and my precious bottles broke on contact with the tarmac.

The PM, who had just disembarked from his Flamingo parked beside me, witnessed my despondency, let alone concern about court martial, walked over to me, opened his top coat, and from its pockets produced two bottles of the same brand.

All he said was, 'Smart thinking, young man. It was the last chance either of us are going to get.'

With that, I knew that my transgression would never be reported beyond the perimeter track of Northolt airfield. The blitzkrieg was on, and I knew that my imminent involvement would pre-empt any disciplinary action.

On 22nd, the squadron was ordered to Hornchurch – a front line battle station.

CHAPTER TWO

The Blooding of Guns

May 23rd, 1940

Twelve Rolls Royce Merlins roared in unison with twelve fighter pilots crouched in their cockpits alone with their thoughts.

This was the day, the hour, the moment of truth. The British Expeditionary Force was retreating towards the Channel Ports, deserted by their French allies.

I watched the plane of my flight commander, Paddy Green, ahead of me and repeated his last instructions to myself: 'Stick to my tail and for God's sake keep a look out behind.'

I had no feeling of fear, just the intense excitement before any contest. The fact that this was to the death, didn't cross my mind. I looked down at Cap Gris Nez, and up at the dark surround of smoke which hung predatorily above it from its source on earth.

Then, 'Look out, 109s,' someone yelled over the intercom, and almost simultaneously I saw it. It was grey and evil-looking with its large black crosses. So, this was it…and as I started after him, I wondered if this was his first combat, as it was mine. If he felt as I did. If he had once loved to fly in peace, rolling and looping in the towering cumulus, high up and alone in clear blue skies. I wondered how soon he would spot me closing in on him, or whether I could take him unawares.

Then suddenly he turned in a tight circle, but I turned tighter. I saw him crouched in his cockpit, looking back at me as I held him in my gun sight and pressed the trigger of my eight machine guns. I saw the flash of my bullets as they struck his wings and tail plane. Then, I heard the bullets thudding in to me and saw his compatriot whizz past. I'd forgotten Paddy's warning to look behind me.

I was angry now, and prepared for a second attack when Paddy's aircraft suddenly appeared in front of me. He hit the 109 with a long burst of fire, and an aileron flew off and fluttered earthwards like an autumn leaf. The aircraft flick rolled, then spewed out its pilot. I was close enough to see his helmet fly off, a white face and blonde hair streaming grotesquely. He didn't pull the rip cord. My petrol gauge was showing next to zero, so I radioed Paddy that I was returning to base and dived towards the ground. I saw the blazing wreck of a Spitfire as I darted seawards over the beach. It was Pat Learmond's – the squadron's first war casualty.

I made Hornchurch with only a few gallons to spare, and as I climbed out of my cockpit, my head ached from the smell of cordite and my heart was hammer-pounding. Some of the others had already landed and were giving their combat reports to the Intelligence Officer. Others were in the circuit. So this was what it was all about, I thought to myself as I walked wearily towards our dispersal hut.

After adding up scores of confirmed and probably destroyed, patching up bullet holes, the squadron took off again in the afternoon, and ran into the enemy as soon as we reached the beaches. A swarm of Heinkels approached like a gaggle of grey geese. Just above them, their close escort of countless Me 110s, and higher still a swarm of 109s, small specks which betrayed their presence by their smoke trails in the sky.

I didn't know how Roger proposed to attack the armada, and I thought of Henry V at Agincourt, perhaps because it was not far from us. Suddenly, Roger's voice broke the RT silence:

'Paddy, your flight take on the top cover. The rest stick with me, and we'll take on the bombers.'

I stuck to Paddy's tail as he scrambled for more altitude, and all of a sudden we were in the middle of a milling mass of Me 110s. I turned in behind the closest of them. He had a shark's jaw painted on his nose. I saw his rear gunner's tracer bullets reaching for me and then stop abruptly as I took aim and fired my first burst from my eight machine guns. On my second, he lurched, flipped over on his back and started to plunge towards the ground, both engines on fire.

The 110s had formed into a defensive circle with the Spitfires wheeling and shooting inside it. Picking their targets, one after the other. The rear gunners fired back. The sky was filled with tracer. A veritable maelstrom of whizzing bullets. I crouched lower in my cockpit to make myself as small a target as possible, tacked on to another 110, and finished the rest of my ammunition into him at about fifty yards' range. I couldn't miss and again I saw the engines start to smoke, then burst into flames as he broke away from the circle.

As I ducked out of this aerial arena since there was no more that

I could contribute, and I had felt several ominous thuds in my fuselage, I heard Roger 'whooping' on the intercom that he had got one, and was after another. Then, minutes later, cussing that some bastard in a Me 109 had got to him.

As I was racing back across the Channel, another Spitfire flew up beside me, and the pilot pulled back the hood and started pointing at my aircraft. Then, Bob Tuck came on the intercom and chortled, 'You look like a sieve, chum.' I scanned his fuselage and answered back, 'Just wait until you get a look at your crate.'

We escorted each other, more slowly, back to Hornchurch. When we had landed we discovered that Roger, John Gillies, the famous plastic surgeon's son, and Sergeant Pilot Paul Klipsch were never to join us again.

Sergeant Paul Klipsch

Paddy Green had landed at Hawkinge, his cockpit awash with blood. He'd been hit in the thigh with an armour-piercing bullet. But according to the pilot's claims of confirmed, probables and damaged, we'd knocked out an awful lot of Luftwaffe, and I myself had witnessed very many tumbling towards the ground. We reckoned we were a very long way ahead of our losses.

The Station Commander, 'Daddy' Bouchier, drove over to our dispersal while Bob Tuck and I were checking who had the most bullet holes in our respective Spitfires, congratulated us and told Bob that he was to take over acting command of the squadron.

Back in the officers' mess, we downed unconscionable pints of beer.

The next day we could only muster eight serviceable aircraft. Crossing the French coast, we ran into about fifty bombers with their fighter screen. Harry Edwards, in the section I had been promoted to lead, and myself took on the close escort Me 110s who turned for home in closed ranks, trying to keep us at bay with their rear gunners. We attacked from beneath their line of fire until our ammunition ran out. Two of my targets went down in flames before the 109s caught up with us...bullets flying everywhere. I ducked for home. As I swept over the beaches, Pete Casanove called me that he'd been shot down and crash-landed. Asked me to call his mother, which I promised I would.

I staggered in to land, my guts aching from the centrifugal forces of air combat, and my right eye was bleeding from a burst blood vessel. My fitter helped me out of the cockpit. My rigger counted eighteen bullet holes in my Spitfire. All the rest of the boys landed safely. Bob Holland with half an aileron, Al a direct hit on his reflector sight, and Tuck, as usual, full of holes.

That evening developed into a party, God knows why. We hadn't much to celebrate except rumours we were being temporarily rested. We had lost our CO, five pilots and Paddy wounded but we wanted to forget the battle and make merry. That was the spirit, initiated at the battle of Dunkirk, which prevailed amongst fighter pilots throughout the war.

The officers' mess suddenly came alive when the station band moved in, and started to play in the dining room, which had a resident piano in one corner. We pulled back the tables and danced with the WAAFs between our prodigious consumption of alcohol.

Bob Holland gobbled his Benzedrine, washed down with whisky, and took over the upright. The band followed for a while, until his feverish tempo became too fast to keep up with. Everyone stopped dancing and gathered around the pianist. Gratuitous drinks appeared in front of him, and he helped himself liberally.

Finally, the party was over, the bar closed, the band dispersed and the weary fighter pilots staggered to their bedrooms. In my dreams, I saw nothing but black crosses, and I was glad when dawn came.

May 25th

We could only field one flight on account of our missing pilots and bullet-riddled aircraft. Bob Tuck led the patrol over Dunkirk. The enemy must have been in the same predicament, or worse, as we only sniffed out one Do 17 which Bob and I shot down between us. We saw two men jump out before the Dornier hit the water, but one parachute failed to open, so, we reckoned the airman dead. We watched the second man float down, wished him luck and headed back to Hornchurch.

Bob Holland, Allan Wright and Sergeant Eyles

Over our first pint in the officers' mess the Station Commander handed us two signals he had just received, one from Keith Park, C in C 11 Group, the second from 'Stuffy' Dowding, as we affectionately called him, the C in C Fighter Command. Both congratulated 92 Squadron pilots on a magnificent performance. He then told us we were leaving for Duxford forthwith to put a new team together under a newly appointed CO.

May 26th

Duxford was a haven of peace, and we needed it badly. All save Bob Tuck who thought it a waste of good shooting time and took some of us out to shoot up German shipping off the enemy-occupied coastline. The rest of the time we basked in spring sunshine and drank beer in the local pub while we gradually unwound and awaited our replacement pilots.

Our new CO 'Judy' Sanders arrived; he was the complete antithesis of Roger, with no combat experience which wasn't his fault. Poor devil, to take on us lot, I thought. Bob Tuck had pulled strings to get his old compadre from 65 Fighter Squadron to take over Paddy Green's flight, and Brian Kingcome moved in with his bulldog 'Zeke'. They looked and acted somewhat alike.

Two other recruits were Geoffrey Wellum and Wimpy Wade. Geoff was 18 years old and very unsure of himself. Wimpy borrowed my Spitfire to get in some more time on the type, and straightaway slow rolled it at nought feet over the airfield, so was forthwith accepted in our league.

During the next week 'Judy' started to exercise his authority as our new CO but it was an unenviable task. We were cock-a-hoop with our substantial victories which had established us as one of the top-scoring fighter squadrons over Dunkirk. We had been lauded by Fighter Command. We just couldn't respect any other leaders than those we had had: Roger Bushell and Bob Tuck. We were a 'bolshie' bunch of bastards, our tails riding high.

The squadron fought its last battle over the Dunkirk beaches on the second day of June We flew to our forward base at Martlesham Heath where two other squadrons were stationed, one commanded by Douglas Bader. In the afternoon we took off as a wing, 92 leading and led by Bob Tuck, our new CO deferring to Bob's combat experience.

It was a comforting spectacle to see a gaggle of thirty-six Spitfires around me. Bob had briefed the wing to fly in loose formations. The Hun was going to have a rude awakening, I was thinking.

We intercepted ten miles behind Dunkirk. The bombers were flying in their formations of threes, and there were lots of them, but their fighter cover appeared quite a way off, for some reason. Bob ordered 92 to go straight for the big boys, and the other squadrons to engage the escort fighters, then ploughed straight on in.

My section, with Harry Edwards, attacked a Vic of three He 111s from below where their rear gunners couldn't reach us. We slid from one to the other, as they started to burn. Then hopped over to a second Vic formation, and repeated the exercise from about a fifty yard range. We silenced all six rear gunners and set five Heinkels on fire, before running out of ammo. Sammy Saunders confirmed that he saw at least three hit the deck, but I didn't stick around when their escort 109s started to get to us.

Back at Hornchurch, we thought we were due to stay either there or Northolt for the big action to follow, and it came as a bomb blast of disbelief and disappointment when we were told that the squadron was being posted to 10 Group in Wales. Maybe Fighter Command thought we'd taken too much of a pounding*, and it would be better

* Killed: Paul Klipsch; Pat Learmond.

Roy Mottram, Brian Kingcome and Sammy Saunders

to have the time to reform our new team in comparative tranquillity and under our new 'unblooded' squadron commander until the finals of the big game they knew was coming.

Wounded: Paddy Green

POW: Roger Bushell; John Gillies; Peter Casanove. Bushell was shot by the Gestapo while leading the Great Escape.

Maybe they were right, but we didn't see it that way.

On June 18th the squadron took off for Pembrey in South Wales. We broke formation over the aerodrome, and buzzed everything in the environment, rudely arousing the Welsh country from its tranquillity. Farmers, doctors, parsons, lawyers, local councillors and police flooded the telephone lines to the Station, demanding an explanation for our demoniacal flying.

I rolled my Spitfire around our new CO, 'Judy' Sanders, my engine cut dead, and I force-landed in a bog which I had mistaken for a field. I skated along on the mud, and started to turn up on my nose. For a moment, I hung poised, terrified that my Spitfire would turn over on its back, and drag me down with it, into the quagmire.

It fell back on its belly, and I leaped out, as it started to sink. I waded out, practically up to my neck in mud and stagnant water, and, on reaching terra firma, was promptly arrested by the Home Guard. Since I was wearing red Daks trousers and an old Stoic tie, my captors were highly suspicious and took me to the local police station where I was locked up.

After a brief incarceration, and an exchange of telephone calls, our Adjutant drove over to claim me. The Station Commander was apoplectic, and had Judy on the mat. He warned him of the unpopularity of fighter pilots, spread by the defeated army on their return from Dunkirk, who blamed their ignominy on the lack of air support.

When we had settled in, and down to convoy and sector patrols, I found time to write to my father in India about Dunkirk.

RAF Pembrey, June 25th, 1940

'Dear Pop: I'm afraid that the fighter boys are in very bad odour at the moment over the Dunkirk evacuation operations. The BEF have started stories that they never saw a single fighter the whole time that they were being bombed. The feeling ran very high at one time, and some fighter pilots got roughed up by the army in pub brawls. Well, whatever you may have heard in India – this is the true story as I saw it over Dunkirk and Calais. Fighter Command were at first disinclined to send the Spitfires out of England at all. We are primarily home defence. Anyhow we went, and at first just as single squadrons (twelve Spitfires). You have had my accounts of how we used to run into 50 and 60 German machines every time we went over there, and fought them until our ammunition ran out. While this battle was going on up at 10,000 feet, the dive bombers which did the chief damage were playing havoc down below us. The fact was that they had layers of bombers and fighters, with which twelve Spitfires had to cope.

'When eventually Fighter Command decided to send over more than one squadron at a time, they forbade us to fly below 15,000 feet.

'We were over Dunkirk on the second last day of the evacuation with more than our squadron. We went over in layers between 15,000 and 25,000 feet. Our squadron led the armada. We disobeyed our orders and came down to 9,000 feet where we ran into thirty He 111's which we drove back, destroying about eighteen of them. However, below us the dive bombers were operating the whole time.

'No wonder the soldiers did not see us up at 10,000 feet but little do they realise that we saved them from the 'real bombs', 500-pounders carried by the Heinkels. What reasons Fighter Command gave for forbidding us to go below 15,000 feet I don't know.

'Here are some alternative suggestions (a) they considered that the navy and troops could deal with low flying dive bombers, (b) The navy shoot at any aircraft which flies near them, no matter what nationality. (c) The navy was confident that it could drive off dive bombers. (d) Fighter Command could not afford to lose too many first line home defence fighters in these operations. A friend of mine was shot down by a cruiser in these operations!

'Well, there is the real story of Dunkirk and the part played by the RAF. One day we shall know the whys and wherefores of the case!!

'This part of the world has been left in comparative peace. We get the occasional raider over here, chiefly at night. We have knocked down two confirmed and about three or four unconfirmed.

Pembrey Dispersal Point

'We heard from Pete Casanove, one of our squadron who was shot down and captured at Dunkirk. He tried to get on three destroyers but was turned off each one. The navy said that all accommodation was reserved for the army, and that the airforce could go f... themselves, gave him a rifle and told him to join the army. Alan Deere, another of my friends, was in the same predicament, but he knocked out the navy man who tried to stop him and got himself aboard. He was middle weight boxing champion of the RAF, a New Zealander, and I guess the others thought it best to leave him alone.

'We were really glad to get our rest. Some of us couldn't eat or sleep much after Dunkirk, but now we are ripe, ready and itching to get back to the action again.

'If I live through this war, I doubt I shall ever be able to settle down to a conventional life. As soon as our wheels touch ground, wine, women and song seems to be the next order of the day. As John Bryson, my best friend, a huge Canadian, ex-Mounted Policeman says, "If the Germans don't kill us, the party at the end of the war certainly will". We know we will win. Love from your son.'

Peter Casanove wrote from his POW camp that he had landed near Paul Klipsch dead in his crashed aircraft, on the Dunkirk beach.* Pete had cut the harness buckle from Paul's parachute, and kept it to return to his parents after the war.

*

July 15th
There was a large TNT factory next to the airfield which had become a Luftwaffe target, and we knew that if they hit it, we would be out of this world. This morning, a cloud-hopping Junkers 88 made a pass at it with a stick of bombs, and I became airborne in a matter of seconds, as I didn't want to be around if they proved to be delayed action.

I cornered him in a cumulus cloud that wasn't quite big enough to hold him, and I chased him in and out of it, like a game of hide and seek. I hit him with several bursts, and his rear gunner hit me, but I couldn't make a kill, and finally he escaped.

The Junkers was a tough one to bring down on account of its radial air-cooled engines, as opposed to the vulnerable liquid-cooled of the Heinkel and Dornier, and a load of armour plating. However, according to one aircraftman who had witnessed the fight and collected some pieces shot off the bomber, "E was very badly 'urt, Sir.'

The populace of Llanelly couldn't understand why he had got away, which, added to the stories they had heard from the Dunkirk soldiery, made the RAF even more unpopular, and several of the boys were barracked in the town.

July 22nd
Brian Kingcome, Bob Holland and John Bryson shot down a Heinkel that had made another pass at the TNT factory, and the townsfolk forgave us.

From the wreck, we salvaged souvenirs of Luger pistols, Leica cameras, Mae Wests and French letters. The boys who boasted that

* In 1982, after some unusual tides causing the shifting of the sand on a Dunkirk beach, the tip of the tailplane of an aircraft was revealed. An excavation proved this to be that of a buried Spitfire, and its number traced through Air Ministry Records to be the one flown by Peter Casanove when he was shot down on May 24th 1940.

they tried out the latter, said they'd rather buy British. We buried the crew with full military honours, and the publican hosted a champagne party for us.

At the beginning of August and to our disgust and despondency A Flight was moved to Bibury and put mainly on night fighter patrols. This was the last straw, when every day we heard on the news what our old friends in 11 Group were doing in the front line.

Bibury was a pretty little Cotswold village, and a great contrast to the sordidness of Llanelly. We were billeted in an old coaching house that belonged to a widow who trained racehorses.

The second day after we arrived, we were attacked, without warning by a Junkers 88. I had just finished a luncheon sandwich, and was watching what I had thought was an Oxford trainer circle the airfield, when, to my horror, it dived down at our dispersal point, machine guns blazing. A stream of bullets ploughed into the ground behind my heels as I dived into a ditch, while a stick of bombs came tumbling out of its belly. I lay mesmerised by the falling projectiles, and could not take my eyes off them until they disappeared into the ground with a succession of mighty crumps when everything was obliterated by smoke and debris. The rear gunner fired a parting burst as the Ju 88 disappeared into cloud.

Pat Patterson, Wimpy Wade and I leapt into our Spitfires, and took off after him. In my haste I omitted my flying helmet, and was, in consequence, out of touch with Ops Room's radio communication which could have directed me in the enemy's pursuit, so I lost him and returned to base.

When I had switched off at my dispersal point and disembarked, I discovered that my flight sergeant had been rapped over the knuckles with a bullet that had first transfixed my aeroplane, two adjacent Spitfires had been written off, and our nearest aerodrome anti-aircraft defence gunner had been shot dead through the heart.

While all this was going on, a light aircraft with two American observers from the US Air Corps was in the circuit. They had only been in England a week, and this was the first action that they had seen. When I greeted them at my dispersal point, the passenger, a Colonel, said, 'Gee, fellah. That baby sure made a pass at us.'

Then, on seeing a number of derelict motor cars which had been dispersed about the airfield as landing obstructions for enemy glider invasion, he added, 'And they sure have made some mess of your transportation.'

Paddy Green, still recuperating from his leg wound, came to visit us, accompanied by Janet (Aitken) Montagu, his love, and Lord Beaverbrook's daughter. A warm, lovely gregarious woman, nine years older than myself, she was to become a life-long, beloved friend and one-time guardian of my first two daughters. She had been twice married. Her first husband, Ian Campbell (Argyll), she had divorced, and the Hon. Drogo Montagu, her second, had spun in an aeroplane to his death.

I had first been introduced to her at Gatwick when she had come over to pick Paddy up for a weekend at her Sussex home, and she invited me to come too. This was in early 1940. But my then flight commander vetoed the invitation.

'Because he's been Bolshie', he said.

'Some other time, then, Bolshie,' Janet had laughed, and I have been called this by the Beaverbrook family ever since.

She had a wide spectrum of friends and she loved fighter pilots, one of which was her brother Max. There was very little she didn't know about Fighter Command from us, and her father, Minister of Aircraft Production, and power behind Churchill.

Her home was warm and hospitable where one could let one's hair down and unwind. She ran her home farm, and drove around in a Railton Terraplane with an enormous Chow dog on the front seat. A bar occupied one corner of her living room, and it was always fully stocked. Beaverbrook heartily disapproved, and on one unheralded visit caught me helping myself liberally, and shouted to his daughter, 'I'll give you a thousand pounds if the bar's been removed by the time I next visit.' It never was.

Many were the times when I retreated to that sanctuary like a hunted animal when I had felt that the war was about to catch up on me, to regain my strength, in order to set forth to fight again.

The squadron's sojourn in the west of the country had not, as we had feared, put us right out of action but Tuck's flight got the cream. Our assignment of protecting a sector encompassing Bristol, Swansea and Cardiff, particularly at night, and on our own, wasn't an easy one. The airfield, so called, at Bibury was nothing more than a landing strip which made night flying, for which a Spitfire hadn't been designed, a most hazardous operation. The only landing lights provided were paraffin flares and Chance light. Once airborne, and out of sight of these, we were entirely dependent upon our radio communication with the Ops Room which vectored us about the pitch-black sky in fruitless efforts to intercept night raiders, and when we were running short of fuel, hopefully back to base. If radio communication broke down, which it had an unhappy habit of doing, you were on your own, and if you couldn't re-locate yourself, you just baled out and hoped for the best.

Norman Hargreaves lost himself, jumped and landed on Martlesham Heath, the other side of England. Sergeant Ronnie Fokes overshot into a brick wall, Geoff Wellum took a wing off on the Chance light, and Tich Havercroft ended up on his back in the middle of the flare path. Later, an 88's rear gunner got him and he crash-landed in Aberdare.

Tich Havercroft

However, by day we added about another dozen to our squadron score with no casualties, although Bob Tuck was shot down twice by rear gunners of Ju 88s which were beginning to prove that they could give almost as good as they could take. He crash-landed on both occasions. At this time, I was beginning to feel that Fighter Command should start re-assessing the power of our eight machine guns against armour plate now being installed in our enemy's bombers. I had seen a Spitfire which had been re-armed with two 20mm cannons and four machine guns, and was convinced that this would be the only answer to the rugged Ju 88, at least. At that time, I never guessed that I was to put my convictions to the test with this radical new armament which a lot of successful fighter pilots had opposed as being unnecessary, and whose opinions my action changed.

September 2nd, 1940

I had been given some leave which I had spent shooting with my uncle in Lincolnshire. The weather had been good, and the game plentiful. I liked shooting better than any other sport, I had decided, whether it be hares or huns. I was feeling a giant refreshed, and I was restless to get back into the big action again, as it was at Dunkirk

My flight had moved back to Pembrey, and my return train from

Lincolnshire ended at Llanelly two hours late. I wanted a strong drink, and I wanted it quick, so I humped my suitcase down to our pub where I knew some of the boys could be found, but there were no familiar faces when I entered the bar, only strange and very dejected ones. I asked the innkeeper's daughter, who was bar-tending, whether any of the boys had been in, and she looked very surprised to see me, and told me the squadron had left for Biggin Hill two days ago; then she added, 'And not 'arf did they get drunk, they did. One of 'em tried to get into my bedroom for a snug and tickle, and the bulldog bit one of our regulars. 'E was as drunk as the rest.'

My God, why hadn't the Adjutant got in touch with me, I first thought, and then I knew. This was going to be my last leave, except for the odd 48 hours that I was going to get, for a very long time.

'Are you one of 92 Squadron?' My thoughts were interrupted by a bleary-eyed flying officer, and when I nodded, he said 'Gone to relieve us at Biggin. Bloody murder up there. We stuck it out for three weeks, until we had only nine pilots left. I reckon you won't last two. They come over in hundreds. Bombers supported by 110s and 109s, in layers from fifteen thousand to thirty-five thousand feet. Bloody swarms of 'em. Lead flying everywhere.' He gesticulated

92 Squadron pilots: *(Back row)* Sebattian Maitland-Thompson, Tom Weiss, Geoffrey Wellum. *(Front row)* Johnnie Kent, self, Bob Holland, Wimpy Wade.

wildly with his tankard, showering me with beer. I knew he was really gone, and pretended I hadn't noticed. 'The airfield's had the shit knocked out of it, and I reckon it's safer in the air.'

Station transport picked me up, after a phone call and another drink, and as soon as I had got back to the Station, I packed the rest of my personal effects, and made arrangements for my air lift to Biggin on the morrow. There was no sign of my Ford V8 Coupe, for which I had traded in my MG on my twenty-first birthday with a parental financial subsidy, so I reckoned one of my friends had assigned himself the responsibility of delivering it to Biggin.

I was too excited to sleep much, and spent most of the night in speculating what the future might hold in store for me. It never entered my head that I could be killed. All I could imagine was shooting the Luftwaffe out of the sky, with the boys beside me, and winning honour and glory for myself and the squadron.

In retrospect, I realise how pathetically naive we were in the supreme confidence of youth which would never countenance any thought or possibility of defeat.

CHAPTER THREE

The Battle of Britain

September 12th

As my Anson transport plane made a quick circuit of Biggin, I had looked at the scene below. The whole environment was a mess of bomb-scarred earth and bombed-out buildings. The hangars were in ruins, the entire airfield pock-marked with bomb holes ringed with obstruction warning flags. There were newly laid patches on the runways where craters had been filled in and tarmacked.

The Anson picked its way cautiously between the obstacles, and taxied up to the nearest dispersal point.

A squadron of Spitfires were dispersed in their pens with starter trolleys and ground crews at readiness. With a surge of excitement I saw the 92 Squadron markings on their fuselages.

The boys, in their flying boots, fur coats and Mae Wests were either standing by their aircraft talking to their ground crews, or lounging in chairs outside the wooden pilots' dispersal hut. Brian's bulldog was sprawled at his master's feet.

The ferry pilot wasn't going to switch off, and gestured me to get moving. He'd seen all he wanted to of Biggin Hill, for sure. No sooner had I humped my baggage out the back of the Anson than it swung around, and took off cross-wind.

The boys helped me stow my gear in the aircrew station wagon while I shot questions at them on the form.

'We shoot at Huns all day, dear boy, and get bestially drunk at night,' Brian answered. 'Station stores has been blitzed, so you can help yourself to anything in the line of flying clothing. I got two of everything for a rainy day.'

As he spoke, the ack-ack guns started barking at a Ju 88 which had emerged momentarily from cloud cover over the airfield heading south, having, evidently, dropped his bombs, as he ignored us.

'What does one do on these occasions?' I asked, a little nervously,

'Just put on a tin hat, and strike a hostile attitude,' Brian said.

Suddenly the Tannoy loud hailer crackled to life: '92 Squadron at 30 minutes available', and the fighter pilots made a concerted dash for the station wagon, which took off packed, with others hanging on to the outside wherever there was a foothold.

'Where's my V8?' I shouted at Brian above the roar of the unsilenced exhaust.

'Sorry about that, chum. Norman drove it into a bus and wrote it off when you were on leave. Had up for drunk driving, but fortunately, the local beak had a son in Fighter Command, and let him off with a pound fine.'

'I'll fix him, for this,' I yelled.

'Been fixed already, poor chap, on the dawn patrol, yesterday,' Brian sighed. 'Tuck's taken over 257 Squadron at Martlesham. Hurricanes, poor sod. Al's got his flight.'

'Guess I'd better check in with the CO,' I said.

'He's out of action. Set himself on fire with his cigarette lighter. Seems someone had cleaned his uniform with a hundred octane,' Brian replied laconically.

Over a NAAFI lunch in the crew room, I asked John Bryson what the action was after dark, and he just winked 'plenty'.

The guns started roaring again, and a stick of bombs crashed across the airfield. Most of us had dived under cover when we had heard the dive bomber coming, except Brian who had remained seated. 'This gives me the most terrible indigestion,' was all he said.

Climbing, self-consciously, back on to my chair, I assumed that this was something that I would have to acclimatise myself to.

The regular officers' mess had been bombed and evacuated, as far as sleeping accommodation was concerned, so we were billeted in an old army establishment, adjacent to which were a number of wooden huts which had been divided into rows of small bedrooms. Having stowed my kit, and met up with my batman, I found Station stores, and helped myself to two of everything, as Brian had advised. I drew another parachute from the section, chatted up a WAAF packer, and made sure that she knew, and had done a good job. By that time, it was almost dark, and the squadron had been released.

As we dined in the old army mess the night bombers started pouring over the airfield in a steady stream, heading for their target, London. Biggin was in their flight path. Their high-pitched, desynchronised engines droned above the yapping of the anti-aircraft guns.

After one large explosion had rocked the building, Johnnie Bryson suggested, 'Let's all get out of here, and watch the bombing from the White Hart at Brasted. Far more fun.'

Wimpy Wade wouldn't be hurried over his dessert, and Allan
Wright declined. He was more interested in processing the war
photographs he took, and reading, we figured. He took the war
quietly, in his stride, unworried. We couldn't level with him. He
liked a party, but only one a week. The rest of us liked one every
night. Having taken over Bob Tuck's flight, Al had a lot of
responsibility. We secretly admired him because we knew that we
needed the alcoholic tranquilliser and stimulant in order to keep
going, all the time, while he relied on his sober self-control, and a
philosophy all his own.

With Allan Wright and Brian Kingcome

The station wagon set off at demoniacal speed, with John Bryson
at the wheel.

'Ninety-two Fighter Squadron,' everybody yelled in unison, as
response to the sentry's challenge, and we swept through the guard
room gates on our way to Brasted.

The White Hart was a typical country pub, with low beamed oak
ceilings. The appendages of hunting horns and horse brasses were
now interspersed with squadron crests and war souvenirs. Two very
tall and identical twins were talking to a short little man with a

goatee beard. They greeted the boys effusively, and Brian introduced me to the MacNeal sisters. Drinks started coming up from all directions, with someone or other's compliments.

'Who's paying for all this?' I asked.

'Don't know, who cares, as long as I'm not. The natives are very friendly,' Brian said.

'What's the scene upstairs?' I asked.

'Plenty to shoot at. They come in their hundreds.'

'Time, gentlemen, please,' yelled the barman.

'Who's for the Red House?' said one of the twins. I couldn't tell the difference. There was a unanimous howl of approval.

And then, I saw her coming down the stairs.

She had honey blond hair down to her shoulders and the bluest of eyes. Her figure was like what most men dreamed about. She seemed preoccupied and unhappy. Her escort was an over-fed army major.

'Who the hell is that one?' I whispered to Brian.

'Not for you, Tony boy. She's army property. A London model. Bombed out of her flat. She's staying down here.'

She passed quite close to me and I could smell her perfume.

'Paula, meet Tony,' one of the twins said. I could only say:

'Hello, Paula.'

'Come on, chaps, let's get up to the Red House,' pleaded someone.

I didn't want to leave her, but I guessed there was no alternative. I hated the army major.

We piled into the station wagon like sardines again, and after a short drive, arrived in front of a fine old red brick manor house. The twins had gone ahead, and were waiting for us at the door. I was shown into the drawing room, and a very large whisky thrust into my hand. Someone put on the radiogram and John Bryson grabbed one of the twins and started to dance her around the floor. He was the only one taller than they were.

Several hours, and three bottles of Scotch later, I suggested that we should be getting back to the airfield. Geoff Wellum had been sick in the garden. Brian said that he was staying on for a while, but I couldn't figure which twin was the attraction. I wondered how we were going to make dawn readiness, but I wondered more about Paula.

September 13th

My batman called me at 4.30 a.m. with a cup of tea. I struggled into my clothes and bumped into Wimpy Wade in the corridor. He had thrown on his uniform over his pyjamas. It was cold and dark outside. The boys converged from various rooms of our barrack block, dressed in polo-necked sweaters, corduroy trousers and flamboyant scarves.

We clambered aboard the station wagon, and started for the dispersal area. No one spoke, and only the shattered exhaust pipe broke the silence.

Our Spitfires stood silhouetted against the backdrop of the dawn sky. In the middle of our dispersal hut stood a pot-bellied stove which had already been lit by the Duty Ops telephone operator. Around the walls, the pilots' cots were distributed, head to toe. I strapped on my Mae West and walked out to my aircraft. My fitter Wallace was sitting in the cockpit making his final check.

'Everything under control?' I asked.

'Yes, sir. Running like a bird. Wouldn't let anyone else fly her. Kept her unserviceable 'til you got back.'

'Good work, Wallace,' I said.

As I strolled back to the dispersal hut, I wondered how much we owed our lives to the devotion of people like Wallace. Our fitters, riggers and armourers.

When I re-entered the crew room, I watched the boys lying on their iron cots in Mae Wests and flying jackets, some tossing in uneasy sleep. Others played nervously with flying helmets and oxygen tubes, or studied enemy aircraft identification charts, and the sector maps pinned to the wooden plank walls. Someone had stuck up a warning poster with black crosses painted on it, and underneath, written *'Remember the Hun in the Sun'*.

The Duty Ops airman was sitting at his corner desk with his hand ready to pick up the direct line to the Controller. Suddenly, the silence was shattered by the roar of an engine starting up the other side of the airfield.

'God, how I hate this waiting. Why don't the buggers come?' someone said. As if in answer, the Ops phone bell broke the silence, and as one man, the pilots were on their feet.

Brian grabbed the instrument and held it to his ear. 'OK, chaps, it's scramble Angels 20, rendezvous with 72* over base.' It was a rush for the door, and a race for our Spitfires, as the Tannoy loud hailer howled the alarm.

* Stationed at Biggin Hill when we arrived.

92 Squadron at Biggin Hill

Twelve pilots leapt into their cockpits and strapped on their parachutes. Twelve Merlin engines of one thousand horsepower coughed and roared into life.

I pushed my throttle open in pursuit of Brian, and the squadron gathered momentum, then launched itself into the air, in close formation. Climbing slowly, in a left hand circuit, we joined up with 72, then reached for the sky, and operational altitude.

I looked down at the earth below. Under my port wing, I could see the River Thames winding through the city of London, the early morning mist enveloping it in a semi-transparent shroud. The rising sun glinted on the myriad of barrage balloons that looked like grotesque fungi sprouting from the ground. I could see no other fighters in the sky, and I thought, there we were, twenty-four Spitfires barring the way to the destruction of the capital city of the British Commonwealth of Nations, by a ruthless enemy. Obviously, the after-effects of the previous night's drinking were still with me.

'Keep up, Red Two,' someone barked on the RT, and I suddenly realised the remark was addressed to me. I had been day-dreaming, and slipped well behind my leader.

Then, 'Hello, Gannic, Leader! Gannic Leader! Carfax calling! 200 plus coming in over Red Queen. Vector 120. Angels 22.'

'Hello, Carfax. Gannic Leader. Message received. Over.'
Brian's voice.

'Hello, Gannic. Gannic Leader. Carfax calling. Watch out for
snappers above. Many snappers above. Hear me?'

'Loud and clear, Carfax. Over and out.'

I looked over my starboard wing, and in the distance, could
make out hundreds of little black puffs of cotton wool in the sky.
They were approaching fast, and travelling in the wake of an armada
of dark bombers flying in V formations.

The 'snappers' were made visible by smoke trails in the sky.
Jeesus, I thought. Where the hell do we start on this lot? I saw six
squadrons of Hurricanes tearing up on our port side and I felt less
lonely.

'Tally Ho, right. Here they come, chaps,' somebody yelled on
the RT, and the squadron swung towards the approaching enemy
which were making straight for London.

'OK, boys, let's go.' Brian half rolled, and tore into the leading
formation from the quarter. I lowered my seat, crouched over my
gun sight, and followed him.

Yours truly

As we closed in on
them, I pushed my
face close to the
armour plated glass,
and tried to make
myself as small as
possible. This was
like the Dunkirk
days. The thrill of the
chase. The scent of
the kill.

I watched as Brian
opened fire. Flames
spurting from his
eight machine gun
ports. I filled my gun sight with a fat Dornier, and pressed the
trigger. My guns started their staccato chatter, and lead crashed into
its fuselage with flashing De Wilde. He jettisoned his bombs, and
started to burn. I transferred my aim to another, and his engine
cowling flew off before I was caught in his slip stream and tossed to
one side as my ammunition ran out.

Simultaneously, my ailerons gave a jolt as one of them was hit, and I saw two 109s flash by.

I yelled, 'Snappers', on the RT, half rolled, and dived for the deck. Aircraft were falling, in every direction, out of the sky which was now full of smoke trails and parachutes.

I made a dicey landing due to my crippled aileron, taxied up to my dispersal point where my apprehensive crew helped me out of my cockpit.

I hurriedly lit a cigarette, before I said anything.

'You all right, Sir?' Wallace asked me anxiously.

'Bit of 109 trouble, that's all. Got my aileron.'

I walked over to the dispersal hut, and slumped down in a chair. Some of the boys had preceded me, and Tom Weiss, our Norwegian Intelligence Officer was trying to get their combat reports. I asked him if all the boys had got back, and he told me that Gus Edwards and Sergeant Eyles hadn't checked in yet. Geoff Wellum said that a Spitfire had spun down quite close to him, in flames, but too fast to get its squadron markings.

Within a couple of hours, my mechanics had fixed my damaged aileron, and shortly after, the Tannoy loud hailer cried out its fateful air raid warning:

'92 Squadron scramble. Angels 20.'

Harry Edwards

High over the cliffs of Dover, we saw them coming in their hundreds. Look left, look right, behind into the sun where the Me 109s always lurked.

'Keep up, Blue Two. Snappers above.'

Back wet with sweat. Breathing faster. The waiting and the watching that is fear. They are near now. Legs strong on rudder pedals, safety catch off, hands firm. Then, 'Tally Ho' from Brian, and the wing over and dive into attack, after one look behind.

Within range, a thumb depresses the trigger button as the enemy fills the gunsight. A backlash of eight machine guns, a reek of cordite in the cockpit, a stream of tracer pouring forward.

A cry over the RT: 'Watch out. Snappers coming down.' Then, the sky full of planes. Twisting. Sniping. A hailstorm of lead. Blinding centrifugal forces. Ammunition gone. Alone and unarmed in a hostile sky. A dive for the deck, and a heading for home. Unsteady landing, and switch off at dispersal point. A welcoming hoist out of the cockpit by mechanics who secretly thought they might not have seen you again. Intelligence reports gabbled to the IO. A count up of score. Five confirmed, and three probables.

'Good show,' from the Station Commander- Group Captain Grice.

'Who's for the White Hart?' somebody shouts, and a spontaneous show of hands, all except Allan Wright's. 'In twenty minutes, then.'

'Time, ladies and gentlemen, please,' called the barman, and a sad silence descended upon the civilian customers as we left the White Hart Inn.

'Get one for me,' said a man with one arm.

'Who's for the Hilden Manor?' Bob Holland shouted. A howl of 'ayes' greeted his suggestion, then a scramble for the station wagon, a roar of its motor and a screech of tyres.

John Bryson drove the station wagon up to the front door of the road-house, and struck a major whom he had failed to see, in the buttocks.

'Why the bloody hell don't you look where you're going?' the soldier shouted.

'Why the hell didn't you get your fat ass out the way?' John shouted back.

'Get out of there, and come inside,' barked the infuriated major.

'He wants to play,' John grinned, as he heaved his six foot four of carcass from under the wheel.

The victim took one look at John, and stalked through the door into the road-house. John followed him up to the bar, and bought him a double whisky. The boys were greeted effusively by some quite pretty hostesses, and the head waiter who asked what our day's score had been while leading us to a prominent table. When we told him, he bowed and said that the drinks would be on the house.

A combo was playing Tuxedo Junction, and couples moving lethargically on the dance floor, as the first bottle of whisky appeared. John had brought the prettiest hostess with him, and after we had helped ourselves liberally to the gratuitous liquor, Bob swallowed a couple of Benzedrine tablets, got up and walked over to the band who had just finished their number.

'Going to play for us tonight, Bob?' asked the pianist, vacating his stool in anticipation.

Bob needed no encouragement. After flying, piano playing was his life. He started with something slow and nostalgic which reminded him of times before the war. Full whisky glasses appeared one by one on the top of the piano, and Bob helped himself with one hand while keeping on playing with the other.

Then, as the Benzedrine started to take effect, his tempo quickened. Sweat had started to pour down his face, and he closed his eyes as he rocked his head from side to side in ecstasy at his music making. Some of the guests stopped dancing, or left their tables to gather around this impromptu performer who helped himself to booze and Benzedrine in turn, and played piano like the greatest. All of a sudden he stopped, grabbed one of the hostesses, and walked her out of the room, through the black-out curtained French Window, into the garden and into the swimming pool. The band resumed their playing, the customers their dancing, and the fighter boys their drinking on the house, until it closed.

*

The first opportunity I had, I located and bought, with parental financial support, a twelve cylinder Lincoln Zephyr coupe. It went for £100, as no civilian could get enough petrol to sustain its voracious consumption.

Bob Holland had a supercharged Bentley, Kingcome had been lent the SS 100 racer which belonged to one of the MacNeal twins, and Wimpy Wade, a Packard convertible. None was licensed or insured, and the local constabulary were fully aware of this omission, and once in a while, a police sergeant would come up to the airfield to remonstrate to our Adjutant who would take him to the bar in the officers' mess to which we were summoned.

After copious drinks and choruses of 'Good old Serg' the reprimand would turn into a warning, not of prosecution, but of the date of the next police road check-up of all unlicensed vehicles.

We filled our cars with 100-octane fuel from the aircraft petrol bowsers, without conscience, and everyone turned a blind eye.

September 18th

I was firing at a Dornier 17 and so pre-occupied with my target that I forgot the cardinal rule of air fighting. *Remember the Hun in the Sun.* I heard a cannon shell explode behind my armour-plated seat back, a bullet whizzed through my helmet, grazing the top of my head and shattering my gun sight, while others punctured my oil and glycol tanks. A 109 flashed by.

Fumes then started to fill my cockpit, and I knew without doubt that I had had it, so I threw open my hood, undid my straps and started to climb over the side. As I braced myself to bale out, I saw my enemy preparing for another attack, and knew it meant suicide to jump with him around. Escaping airmen over their own territory were fair game in some combatants' log book, and a friend of mine had been shot down in his parachute. So, I decided to bluff it out, climbed back into my aircraft, and turned on my attacker.

My ruse worked; he didn't know how hard he'd hit me, but he did know that a Spitfire could turn inside a Messerschmitt, and I fired a random burst to remind him, whereupon he fled for home. By this time I was too low to jump, so I headed for a field and prayed.

At a hundred feet, my engine blew up, and I was blinded by oil. I hit the ground, was catapulted out, and landed in a haystack, unharmed. I hit the buckle of my parachute to release it, and as it fell to the ground, the pack burst open spewing forth the silk which had been shredded by splinters of cannon shell. I said a hasty prayer before the first of the rescue party could reach me.

I was soon surrounded by a crowd of farmers, and inmates from a public house near by. I asked them where I was, and they told me Appledore, before sitting me on a stool at the bar counter with a first pint of beer. Five pints later, an army officer turned up in a jeep with a couple of Military Policemen. He drove me to his Command Post, where I was given a large whisky. The Commander told me that the

Gaskell, Lund, Wade, Mottram and Kingcome

Dornier had crashed with no survivors.

From there, I was taken to the office of the Chief Constable of Kent who opened a bottle of sherry which we drank before he gave me lunch. I slept the entire journey back to Biggin where I was driven by a very large police officer in a very fast squad car. He delivered me to the officers' mess with the remains of my parachute and demanded a receipt for me from the Adjutant.

The boys then broke the news that Roy Mottram had been killed and Bob Holland wounded. We drowned our sorrows, and John Bryson and Kingcome carried me to bed.

Letter to my mother. RAF Biggin Hill – September 19th, 1940.

'As you will have guessed we have been desperately busy since we have been here – taking a leading part in nearly all the fighting. Of course, we have had our casualties which are only to be expected. Gus Edwards and Norman Hargreaves are still missing and several of the boys are in hospital with wounds.

'I got three more bombers, but yesterday I was shot down by a Me 109 which crept up behind me while I was blowing up a Do 17. I crashed near Dungeness, but thank God I was unhurt, and am ready for anything again now.

'The German Air Force are doing their utmost to smash us. We certainly know that we are up against it, but the morale of the Fighter boys is terrific – We will crack the German Air Force, at all costs. This is our greatest and diciest hour, but we are proud to have the chance to deal with it.

'Please on no account worry about me – I am safe until my predestined time runs out. I am happy, and almost enjoying myself. In these times of danger one gets drawn much closer to one's friends, and a great spiritual feeling of comradeship and love envelops every one. I can't explain, but everyone seems a much better man, somehow –

'I met Chris* in London and we spent the night at the Regent Palace Hotel. The bombing proved only a distraction and we found a bottle of gin far more fortifying than an air-raid shelter. The Londoners, although deadly tired, are standing up to it well, and are full of determination to see things through. Tony.'

*

* My doctor brother, now- senior physician at St Thomas's Hospital, London.

Although I had made very strong resolutions not to get in front of an Me 109 again, I was shot up by one a couple of days later. We were mixing it with a bunch of them, when a salvo of lead crashed into my fuselage behind my armour-plating. I didn't even see my opponent who must have been a pretty good sportsman, as I was doing aerobatics when he hit me. I may even have flown through a stream of bullets that had been aimed at somebody else.

However, when my control column wouldn't respond how I wanted it to, I rolled out of the conflict, found a friendly layer of cloud and set a compass course vaguely in the direction of where I thought Biggin Hill was, scarcely daring to sneeze in case I broke the last of the tail plane cables which I knew had been hit.

When I broke cloud at 800 feet, I had made up my mind to jump, as my engine was beginning to lose power, but I found myself right over Sevenoaks where I dared not jettison my Spitfire for fear of the destruction it might cause in the built-up area. By the time I had passed it, I was too low to bale out, so it was Biggin or bust.

When I made my landing approach, I found this could only be achieved by winding the tail trimming tab fully forward to depress the nose, and control this tendency by easing back on the 'stick', which had lost its forward effect.

I motored in slowly, sweating profusely, and made a pretty commendable landing.

As I turned at the end of the runway and headed towards my dispersal point, I yanked back on the control column, and the last cable broke.

A somewhat bizarre arrangement had been made with the factory where our Spitfires were built. When a pilot assessed that his aircraft was shot up badly enough to necessitate a crash landing, he was encouraged to crash on the factory airfield instead of his own, and pick up a new aircraft from the production line. Another unorthodox arrangement had been established with the Luftwaffe. We had mutually organised a radio communications system whereby we could each report to one another the position of our respective pilots shot down in the Channel. It was the responsibility of whichever Air Sea Rescue boat was closest, to pick up the airmen before they drowned. No one shot at Air Sea Rescue boats – an unwritten law which I experienced three miles off Calais when I took part in a successful Air Sea Rescue operation of one of my pilots.

I wondered what the others felt when they saw the tracer and the black crosses. We never discussed it. John Bryson, whose main thoughts seemed focused on having a good time with girls. The huge, wise-cracking ex-Canadian Mountie who had become my best friend. His dismissal from his previous Service, according to his account, was due to progress in the shape of helicopters. Lonesome, stationed in some North Canadian outpost, he had moved in a couple of Eskimo babes, and was teaching them to play ice hockey when the Commandant literally descended upon them.

Brian was a bit of an enigma. He loved his dog and one of the twins which took up all his spare time.

Bob Holland had his piano and his benzedrine. Al Wright, his letter writing and photos. He and Pat Learmond had shared their love for the same girl. Now Pat was dead, leaving Al a clear field.

Wimpy was an atheist who loved flying and himself, but nice withall. Geoff Wellum, we nicknamed 'the boy'. A youngster who fought and drank as hard as any of us.

From an hour before dawn until dusk we lived at our dispersal point on the airfield, and fought until we ran out of ammunition. At night we drank and played and made love like there was no hereafter. I can't remember all the pilots who flew with us. Some came in the morning and were dead by nightfall. The Biggin Hill Chapel keeps the record. I swore never to hate anyone again after I'd seen one of our team I loathed blow up beside me when caught by a 109. First, Norman Hargreaves had gone, then Sergeant Eyles. Gus Edwards was found dead a week after he went missing, in the middle of a forest. Similarly, Howard Hill, after three weeks, lodged in the top of a tall tree, decomposing in his cockpit, his hands on the controls and the top of his head blown off by a cannon shell. Pat Patterson, though badly burned in a previous escape, refused to be grounded. I saw him spin down quite close to me, having been hit and struggling to get out of his blazing cockpit. A burned offering to the God of War.

After Judy's accident followed two replacement CO's with no previous combat experience who flew number two to Brian in consequence: Lister had won a DFC on the North-West Frontier; McLoughlan, from Training Command. Neither lasted much more than a week being shot down in quick succession. This was no game for inexperience, and Brian continued to lead the squadron with no promotion.

Brian was the only one of us who seemed unaffected by the war.

We would have happily accepted a rest if it had been offered us. Maybe it was, and he never told us. His private life revolved around the White Hart Inn and the Red House of the twins.

The war in the air seemed just an incidental interruption which kept him occupied during the day. He appeared unmoved by our casualties. He seemed to take it for granted. A complete enigma to us who loved and followed him, with complete faith in his leadership. When we had lost one of our sergeant pilots, and one of us asked what became of him, Brian answered, 'Lee's a cinder' which I remember to this day.

*

On his way to Chequers, Churchill would pay us a visit from time to time. He would burst into our crew room, unheralded, and sit and chat with us while he puffed on a huge cigar. He was an honorary air commodore of an Auxiliary squadron, an inspiration, and we were proud to think of him as a friend as well as our leader.

*

John Bryson

On September 24th John Bryson was shot up in a dogfight, but managed, how I'll never know, to land on North Weald airfield. When the ground crew lifted him out of his cockpit, they found him dead. One leg had been blown off just below the knee.

I didn't remember much of John's funeral. I got so drunk that I wouldn't. But I do remember one of the pilot boys, drunker than I was, giving his farewell salute beside the grave, then falling into it.

*

Some days, we could only field five serviceable aircraft out of twelve. We fought all day, and played most of the night. We lived for the present and dismissed our future. The battle would be won, of course. We had no doubts about that. Meanwhile, the casualties mounted, but no one grieved as we knew it was inevitable. I found myself secretly watching the others, searching their faces for who would be next, and I thought I saw them looking at me the same way. But we never revealed our thoughts about fear. They were locked up as tight as the straps on our parachutes.

On September 30th Al Wright was shot down and wounded, and Bob Holland took over as B Flight Commander.

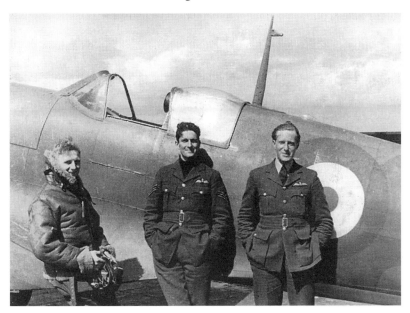

Allan Wright, Sergeant Eyles and Bob Holland

I had developed a septic wisdom tooth which had to be extracted. The dentist was afraid to give me gas because there was too much alcohol in my system, and had to go very easy on the local anaesthetic.

For twenty-four hours, I lay on my bed and spat blood. Then I went up and fought again, and that night something snapped, and for the first time I was really afraid. I drank half a bottle of brandy at the White Hart, and finished it off at the Red House. The twins took me upstairs, and put me to bed. My head was swimming, and I wept like a child, with fatigue and sorrow for the friends I had lost.

The next day, the MO grounded me, and two days later Brian and I heard that we had been awarded the DFC. I went down to my tailor to have it sewn on, and he refused to accept payment. He shook my hand warmly, and as I stepped out onto the pavement, I felt supremely conscious of the blue and purple striped decoration under my wings.

As I made my way to my parked car, pedestrians looked, stopped and then smiled. A young girl stranger ran up and kissed me.

The public wanted to shake our hands, touch us, idolise us. Years later in Hollywood, I saw similar adulation lavished on movie stars who had avoided the draft as homosexuals and conscientious objectors.

Brian told me that I was to take seven days' leave, no argument, and furthermore, that the twins were throwing a party for us at the White Hart, that evening. When I walked into the bar, I saw Bob Holland talking to Paula. She was looking even more beautiful, vulnerable and desirable than the first time I had seen her. When I joined them, she said softly, 'Congratulations, Tony.'

Before I could find words to respond, the twins joined us, and one of them thrust a large whisky into my hand. Then suddenly, the place seemed to become inundated with friends wanting to shake my hand, when all I wanted was to hold her close to me, and kiss those lips.

Inevitably, at closing time, the party moved up to the Red House where someone put on the record player. I asked her to dance, took her in my arms, and immediately forgot the war.

The next morning, I filled up my Lincoln Zephyr with 100 Octane petrol from the squadron bowser, and drove like one possessed to my home in Buckinghamshire. On my arrival, my mother hugged me, and with tears in her eyes, told me this was the proudest moment of her life, but I knew how much she had suffered on my account, reading daily, the newspapers, and listening to the wireless news of the battle being fought for Britain, knowing the part I was playing in it. But she didn't want to ask about it, and I wouldn't have wished to tell her. All I wanted was to forget.

It soon got around that I was home on leave, and people from the village came to call and congratulate. The vicar took a glass of sherry with us, and said he'd see me in church on Sunday, of course. A command performance.

The next morning I drove over to Stowe, and paid my first call on my old headmaster, J.F. Roxburgh, who added his congratulations, but seemed to take for granted what I had won, as he had previously done in my winning my first fifteen rugby football colours. I lunched in the masters' common room where my former tutors were equally congratulatory, and David Brown, my former rugby coach who had captained Scotland, said he'd just lost the Stowe left wing three-quarter by injury, and told me I would be the replacement in the afternoon match against Middlesex Hospital. I thought he was kidding, but he wasn't, and I found myself trotting out onto the familiar ground with the Stowe team, and wearing the familiar school colours.

The air was crisp and smelt of Autumn, and all I now wanted was to relive my school life again, and recapture some of its former happy memories. Fortunately, it turned out to be not a very taxing game on my wing, but what action came my way proved that I could still stop my opponent and beat him to my scoring touch line. Rumour quickly spread amongst the spectators that the rather breathless substitute wing three-quarter was an old Stoic veteran of the Battle of Britain, and everything I did, from then on, whether good, bad or indifferent, was greeted with cheers.

After a few days of leave I started to get restless, and I rang up the Adjutant to find out how the boys were doing. He told me that Bill Williams and John Drummond had been killed, but declined to elaborate. I decided to return to Biggin that afternoon, and my mother didn't try to stop me. She had tears in her eyes as she kissed me goodbye, and looked suddenly old.

'Come back soon,' she whispered, and I was gone.

The boys were in the depth of depression when I checked in at our dispersal point, and told me the gloomy story. Bill, John Drummond and Sergeant Ellis were attacking a Dornier when Bill and Drummond had collided in mid-air. Ellis had witnessed the collision before being hit by the rear gunner and force-landed. Both aeroplanes had blown up, and Bill had fallen near a church with a streaming parachute, where a priest had given him the last sacrament before he died in his arms.

The bombing of Biggin Hill continued sporadically, and the Station Commander decided that the pilots should not sleep at the airfield. He wanted us dispersed, as our Spitfires were. He was concerned about the concentration of pilots. He didn't want all his eggs in one basket, as he succinctly put it.

The Adjutant found us a country house four miles from the airfield, and closer to the White Hart. 74 Squadron who had replaced 72 on October 15th were moved to other sleeping accommodation, in a different direction. The sergeant pilots went elsewhere.

We crated in a supply of liquor that would last us over Christmas, and a four piece jazz band made up of conscripts from the London night clubs. Officially, they were attached to the squadron as aircraftmen second class, by a Personnel Officer at Fighter Command, a friend of our Adjutant, and were forthwith delegated to our billet for general duties. They brought their musical instruments with them.

'Mac', Adjutant of 92 Squadron

CHAPTER FOUR

The Fighting Sergeants

Just as our destroyed Spitfires were replaced with others, so were dead men's shoes refilled with raw young recruits. If they lasted, they gradually got incorporated in our team. Many of them only lasted a few days before they died. Some never returned from their very first sortie. We never even remembered their names.

Quite a number were sergeant pilots of every nationality. They fought with our team by day, but were segregated by rank from us when off duty. An anachronism of our Service. We were all one breed of fighting men.

Don Kingaby was one of these whose companionship I would have cultivated, had I the chance, amongst others, but there was little opportunity, the way we were forced to live. He joined Brian Kingcome's flight of which I was a member.

Sergeant Pilot Don Kingaby got off the London train at Bromley South and boarded a bus on the last leg of his journey to Biggin where he'd been posted to join 92 Squadron. At Leaves Green, a village at the bottom of the hill, the conductress chirped out a cheery 'All change', and in answer to his query, pointed the way up the road leading towards the airfield. The buses had given up driving past the camp since the recent bombings, and this one was no exception. It turned around and hastily departed in the direction from which it had come. Don hoisted his kitbag and set off towards his destination.

Upon reaching it Don found a scene of complete desolation, and one weary-looking aircraftman who directed him to a shattered building bearing the sign 'Sergeants' Mess' beyond the wreckage of a hangar. As he approached it, he heard overhead the sound of unfamiliar aero engines, and looking up, spotted a Ju 88.

Don jumped into a convenient ditch and watched the aircraft make its run over the airfield, then turn and head south. Obviously on a photograph reconnaissance job, he reckoned. Then, he emerged from his cover and continued his hike. On entering the Mess, he found it deserted, but located a telephone, called 92 Squadron Orderly Room and reported his arrival. A voice told him to check in next morning.

It was getting dark when pilots started to arrive from the squadron dispersal points, and a flight sergeant greeted him, and showed him to a room which he was to share with two other pilots. After further introductions, a couple of beers and a hasty supper, most of the pilots took off for their local pub, but weary after his journey, Don decided to turn in early.

At what hour he knew not, he was rudely awoken by an ear-shattering bang, quickly followed by two others, jumped out of bed and started reaching for his clothes. Desynchronised motors droned overhead.

Don Kingaby

'Only ack-ack' came a drowsy voice from the bed next to him. 'Go back to sleep. You're going to need it.'

The gun battery kept up its infernal racket all night long. The building shook, and the windows rattled. Every now and again came the whistling of descending bombs followed by their bursts to add to the cacophony of noise. Not another wink of sleep did he get that night as he listened, and wondered at the composed slumber of his room mates who appeared to accept the holocaust as par for the course.

At dawn, Don reported at the squadron dispersal with two other pilots who had just arrived. They had already collected parachutes. One of the flight commanders interviewed them in the pilots' crew room.

'Have you ever seen a Hun?' he asked.

'No,' replied a sandy-haired lad beside Don.

'Yes,' Don and the third of the trio said simultaneously. His name was Bowen-Morris.

'Have you ever fired at a Hun?' the flight commander added.

'Only once,' Don and Bowen-Morris replied, again in unison.

'Ye gods,' exclaimed the flight commander to the pilots lounging at readiness. 'They've sent us a couple of veterans,' and thus was their introduction to Brian Kingcome.

Don Kingaby had noticed another flight lieutenant in the crew room with the most terrible blood-shot eyes and a crimson face. 'Jesus,' he thought, 'there's a real booze hound, if ever I saw one. Hope I'm not in his flight.' He wasn't, and learned later that the pilot was New Zealander Pat Patterson who had been shot down in flames a few days previously, but refused to take a rest because of the shortage of pilots.

Don put on his overalls and Mae West, sorted out helmet and gloves and picked up his parachute. Brian Kingcome led him out to the Spitfire he was to fly and showed him how to stow his gear, arrange his straps for a quick getaway and introduced him to his ground crew upon whom his life would partly depend. Returning to the crew room he was introduced to his section leader who told him he'd fly his number 3, to stick with him, and always remember the 'Hun in the Sun'.

The rest of the fighter pilots were lounging in chairs or trying to catch up on lost sleep on iron beds scattered around the floor. The Ops telephone rang from time to time as the Sector Controller checked on the aircraft and pilot readiness state, and each time the boys would open a sleepy eye, and cock an ear to the Ops clerk, Aircraftman Webber, who would sooner or later order a 'scramble'. When the phone was returned to its cradle, silence would return, only interrupted by the stertorous breathing of Brian's massive bulldog as he dreamed of despatch riders, his *bêtes noirs* and as soon as they delivered at the dispersal point, they would beat a hasty retreat before Zeke could get his teeth into a leg. Until, one time, he fastened on to a hot exhaust pipe which discouraged further attacks.

The Ops phone rang once more, but this time Webber shouted, 'Scramble Maidstone, Angels Fifteen.'

The pilots hurled themselves from bed and chair, with a mad rush for the open door. Some, whose aircraft were dispersed nearby made them running. Others, parked at some distance, hopped aboard the squadron truck which whisked them to their destination. The Tannoy blared out the 'scramble' alarm. Tongues of flame and belches of blue smoke burst from the Spitfire's exhausts.

Tense and apprehensive, Don clambered up the wing root and

into the cockpit. By the time he was strapped in, some of the others were taxying out, and he panicked in fear of missing his section leader's aircraft, before he spotted him waiting for him, and took up his position. The squadron lined up across the airfield in battle formation, then opened up, and started to roll forwards together; then they were airborne, clearing Biggin's last remaining hangar with a few feet to spare.

Ninety-two were still using the standard Vic formation which Douglas Bader and Sailor Malan had discarded in favour of the 'four finger' concept. Don had been delegated as one of the two 'weavers' to protect the squadron's rear. 'Arse-end Charlies', they were dubbed, and the most precarious position in the squadron. The squadron climbed over Maidstone to fifteen thousand feet; then we were ordered to twenty-five where we reached vapour trail height.

'Sailor' Malan

'Smoke trails, Gannic Leader', a voice came over the RT and Brian, who was leading, eased down out of the treacherous zone which would betray our position to the enemy.

'Hello, Gannic Leader.' The voice of the Controller came over the RT. 'I have some trade for you. Twenty plus bandits with many snappers heading for Red King, Angels twenty. Over.'

'Roger,' Brian answered, and turned south-east. Then suddenly:

'Gannic Leader. Bandits now over Red King. Watch out for many snappers above.'

'Gannic Leader, I see them. Tally-ho, and over.'

Don saw the black puffs of flak reaching for the sky over Dover, then their target, small compact dots constituting the bomber formation. His weaving became more violent as he set himself to guard, not only the tail of the squadron, but his own. The gap between pursuers and pursued was quickly closing, and then Brian's section, wide opening their taps, dived into their attack on the dark grey fat bombers, followed by Pat Patterson's.

Don saw their 109 escort coming down, and shouting a warning. Then all was a maelstrom of fighting aeroplanes. He saw a spurt of flame emerge from Patterson's fuselage in front of his cockpit, and then it blossom into an all consuming fire ball as the aircraft fell away. Then his number two followed, streaming thick black smoke.

Don attacked one of a Vic of three Dorniers. He saw his de Wilde bullets flickering on wings and body as he glued his finger to the trigger button. Then he saw the tracer bullets zipping past his starboard wing as the 109s came down on their prey, and swung into a tight turn which temporarily blacked him out. When his sight returned he found himself on the tail of one of four, closed the gap and finished his ammunition on it, again seeing the de Wilde bullets as they peppered his enemy's wings and fuselage, which started to smoke. Then he flick-rolled and dived out of the combat arena, towards mother earth.

On his landing back at Biggin, Don's ground crew greeted him with eager questions on seeing that the canvas patches over his gunports had been shot away.

'Did you get one, Serg? How many? What were they?'

Don answered that he could possibly claim a 109, and they started to regale him with the news from the other pilots who had landed.

'Mister Kingcome got another one, and Mister Bartley a Ju 88.'

The squadron claims were an assorted bag of six, and another four were claimed by 72. Pat Patterson had been reported killed, and two 92 Spitfires missing. One of them was Wimpy Wade's who turned up by car later. He had taken on a formation of Dorniers, and after hitting one, had been caught in their rear gunner's cross-fire and forced landed on Lewis race track with a punctured radiator.

Sergeant Pilot 'Tich' Havercroft, even smaller than Don, seated himself at the battered crew room piano, and started to play 'boogi' to relieve the tension every one was feeling. He wasn't very adept and the boys shouted at him to make room for Bob Holland who took over with his magic touch.

Mid-afternoon the Ops telephone again gave the alarm, but Brian had stood Don down. Newcomers were treated leniently. Don watched the squadron scramble, then the sirens started their wailing, and the Ack-Ack cracking. He would have gone to earth but for the casual conduct of Flight Sergeant Stewart and Sergeant 'Tubby' Back, armourer and mechanic, who stood their ground, looking skywards for the approaching enemy.

Don watched, fascinated, a formation of Ju 88s with their fighter escort approach remorselessly overhead, then 92 and 66 (our sister squadron) tear into them. The formation started to break up and scatter all over the sky. A lone 88 passed low overhead with a Spitfire close on its tail, firing a continuous burst from its eight machine guns. From its letter on the fuselage, he knew it was Tommy Lund's. The bomber started to shed bits and pieces, then dive towards the ground beyond the airfield perimeter.

The long waiting at 'readiness' in our crew room was full of tension which we tried to relieve with cat-napping, play and shop talk, and interminable squadron tactics. In respect of the latter, two things had been worrying us. The first was the vulnerability of our 'weavers', and Don Kingaby who was in Brian's and my flight seemed invariably to get this precarious job, shared with Tich Havercroft, and in an unexpected manoeuvre both were liable to become separated from the squadron and priority targets for the 109s.

Don suggested that, instead, they should weave in front where they could do their job just as well, and stick with the group, which was agreed. It worked well, and was, thereafter, adopted as a standard operational procedure.

A further consideration was the practicality of flying with the cockpit hood open, two arguments being advanced in favour of this. One, that the reflections from the perspex were distracting, and the other that speck of dirt on it could be mistaken for an enemy fighter and give a false alarm. But an even more compelling reason was that we had found it exceedingly difficult to open the hood at high speed, and there was no jettison mechanism on it, causing a predominant feeling that one could become trapped in a burning cockpit, the fighter pilot's greatest fear. This sticking hood problem exercised the inventive talents of Sergeant Ronnie Fokes, and together with the squadron engineer officer and a senior flight mechanic, the first hood jettisoning mechanism was developed and incorporated in all our aircraft, without reference to the designers or the bureaucrats at the Air Ministry.

CHAPTER FIVE

The Changing Tide

As October dawned, the enemy's day-time activity took shape in fighter sweeps of 109s carrying bombs to drop indiscriminately on London, and dogfights became the order of the day. These began after a scramble for altitude, to get above our enemy and attack from out of the sun from the Spitfire's maximum height.

Brian Kingcome, as acting CO, continued to lead the squadron and quickly twigged the right tactics for meeting the 109 sweeps. Instead of allowing us to be vectored by the ground control directly towards and underneath the enemy he would lead us away to the north-west of London gaining height to 30,000 feet before turning over Kent to meet them. This got us above most of the 109s but did not give complete immunity from them as they had the edge on the Spitfire for ultimate height, and we still had to contend with the menace from their high cover squadrons.

Nearly every patrol was at high level in bitterly cold skies and two more frustrating phenomena developed in the Spitfire's cockpit. Firstly, the inside of the perspex canopy would mist up, and then freeze over, blocking one's efforts to see the enemy fighters and leaving us semi-blinded to their voracious attacks. Frantically one would scrub the ice away and try to peer out, but as fast as it was cleared it would form again and remain there until lower levels were reached. Secondly, when we did see Huns beneath and dived down on them we found that if the dive was a long one, by the time we reached the target the front windscreen would be iced over, completely blocking our view through the gun-sight.

Squadron inventiveness again came to the rescue. It was noticed that if the very small ventilation hatch on the starboard side of the cockpit was open, then the misting was not so bad. The plumbers went to work and led a pipe from the open hatch to the front windscreen where it ended in a fish-tail, splaying cold air on the panel in front of the gunsight. This was effective in clearing a small portion of the front windscreen, just enough to sight through, and although it meant we would be colder than ever we gladly accepted the small tactical advantage it gave us.

Between 7th and 11th October the squadron flew three or four times a day against the 109s and minor brief but fierce encounters took place. On the 12th our first sortie was one of the new 'umbrella' patrols instituted by 11 Group. This was a standing patrol at squadron strength, usually centred on Maidstone at fifteen thousand feet, whether or not there was enemy activity. The idea was to have something ready and waiting for the Hun instead of sitting on the ground at readiness to scramble and intercept.

The squadron was beginning to feel the strain of the last thirty days, and the loss of our friends had a depressing effect upon the remaining few members of the original squadron. Bobby Tuck, taking time off from his new Hurricane squadron, would visit us infrequently to 'shoot the breeze' and see how we were getting along without him. The same old Tuck, full of action and confidence. His score was nearly twenty, and he had won a bar to his DFC.

By the middle of October 72 Squadron had been shot to bits and sent North for a rest, and 74 had taken their place, under the command of 'Sailor' Malan. The Sailor was a South African, as my first CO had been, and on the exterior, tough as nails, but beneath it, very sensitive. 74 were fresh compared to us, and started shooting down Huns, right left and centre. Sailor had already become a leading 'ace'.

The bulwark of their team consisted of their CO, their flight commanders Mungo-Park and Johnnie Freeborn and Flying Officer Harbourne Mackay Stephen. They were all red hot shots, and the squadron the complete antithesis of 92. They did not indulge themselves in large cars, night clubs or fancy dress.

'I kick their arses once a day, and I've got a good squadron. Otherwise they'd wind up nothing,' Sailor told me, and that he'd learned that in the Merchant Navy, in which he'd served before the Air Force. Hence, his nickname.

'Take on four, but run from more,' was another edict.

He considered us just a bunch of playboys, and kept his squadron as distant from ours as possible.

Bob Holland and Roy Mottram were shot down and wounded a few days after 74 had joined us, and I was glad that, at least, two of the boys were safely out of action for the time being. Pancho Villa, from 74, moved over to take command of Bob's flight.

'Tiny' Kinder, a massive New Zealander who had the greatest

Mungo-Park and H M Stephen

difficulty in fitting himself into the Spitfire's cockpit, clobbered a
Ju 87 over Eastchurch, and was then shot down by an escort 109.
His combat report was typical of him, and notwithstanding he'd
been badly wounded, provoked much laughter from the pilots
when IO Tom Weiss read it to us. After describing his successful
attack, it ended.

'Then unfortunately my attention was diverted from another 87
by a cannon shell passing through my right arm, and I was obliged
to force land.'

Another ribald scene concerned Sammy Saunders. Very tall, thin
and rather older than most of us, he was always imperturbable, and
had a quiet sense of humour. He had landed with a shattered canopy,
walked into the crew room, and enquired whether anyone had a
spare helmet he could borrow. Whereupon, he thrust his fist through

a four inch gash in the
crown of his, threw it in a
corner and with his scarf
made a temporary bandage
to staunch the blood
oozing from a large crease
in his cranium.

On October 15th, Brian
was shot down near
Chatham. He was returning
from a skirmish with some
109s, and, to quote his own
words, quite pleased with
his shooting, and only
thinking of a pint of beer,
when somebody shot him.

'Tiny' Kinder

He always swears that it was one of our side, by mistake, and I
recollect the bullet they extracted from his leg proved it.

His aircraft caught fire, and he baled out, landing in a ploughed
field, semi-conscious through loss of blood. A crowd quickly
collected around him, and an army officer produced his hip flask and
offered him a drink. Brian took a swallow, and on discovering it was
water, straightaway fainted.

The bullet was removed at Farnborough Hospital, and the same
evening, some of the boys, the twins and myself went to visit, armed
with liquor. The airfield was only three miles away. A party was held
by his bedside, and Brian got splendidly drunk, but the nurses had
already adopted him, and in their eyes, he could do no wrong. To
describe this action in Brian's own words:

> I was wearing a German Mae West (looted from the
> same Ju 88 we shot down in South Wales) and
> remember watching peasants with pitchforks gathering
> in a group below me as I floated down in my parachute
> and getting a bit worried in case I was mistaken for a
> Hun. There had been some nasty incidents when an
> indignant population had beaten up a few of our chaps
> convinced that they were Germans, but luckily in my
> case they had seen my Spitfire land before me.
>
> I had been shot through the leg, and the friendly
> locals asked me which hospital I fancied. What do you

have? I asked. They mentioned one or two, amongst them the Royal Naval Hospital at Greenwich. Obviously the best choice, I thought in my ignorance, assuming that they would know all about bullet wounds, and opted for there. They duly operated on my leg to remove the bullet, and I came to in bed with my leg in plaster from the waist down. A theatre sister was sitting by the bed, and informed me that I was very lucky to be alive. Apparently the surgeon who operated on me had last been in action when he removed an arrow from someone at the battle of Hastings. He didn't think to X-ray my leg, but had tried to find the bullet by groping up through the path he thought it had probably taken, severed a couple of important blood vessels en route, groped up and down to try and find the ends to tie them off, hadn't found them either, so stuffed a whole lot of gauze into the by now huge wound in the back of my leg, wrapped the whole thing in plaster and told everyone to keep their fingers crossed. It would either stop bleeding or it wouldn't. Luckily it did. So I had myself removed to Orpington Hospital, where a clued up young chap X-rayed my leg, found the bullet was resting just under the skin between the two bones in the front of my leg, and removed it in five minutes with a half inch incision.

Bob Tuck had telephoned Brian at the hospital when he was up and about on his crutches, and they had made a rendezvous at squadron dispersal, determined to fly a sortie together for old times' sake. Bob flew down in his Hurricane, and one of the boys collected Brian from the hospital. Brian jettisoned his crutches, and the ground crew lifted him into a Spitfire, whereupon both took off while the rest of us watched with some trepidation. Bob was in my aircraft.

It so happened that a cloud-hopping bomber was in the vicinity and its position revealed by the bursting of the Ack-Ack shells. We monitored the action on an RT set, and heard a 'Whoopee' of triumph, when they shot it down.

By now Fighter Command had got wind of the 92nd Night Club and sent an RAF psychologist down to Biggin to check our habits. Having spent three days with us, his recommendation was to let us live the way we wanted, since to interfere at this critical stage could be catastrophic. We were shooting down aeroplanes which was all that mattered, and how we went about it was our affair. He doubted, however, if we could keep up our pace for very much longer. At this point Fighter Command was determined to give us a squadron commander who would stick, and Johnnie Kent, a tough Canadian, had been selected.

When Kent was posted to command the squadron, 92 had made about the highest score in Fighter Command. He had been a flight commander in the famous Polish squadron 303, and already held a DFC, an AFC and the *Virtuti Militari*. We didn't take much more notice of John than we had of our two previous CO's and he spent most of his time in the office when he wasn't flying, which suited us fine. No one had done any of the squadron paper work in two months, and unanswered correspondence and unfilled forms were piled high.

Johnnie Kent

Then one morning Johnnie summoned his senior NCO's and pilots to his office. The interview went something like this: 'I have been watching the squadron's action for the past three weeks and all I can say is, it stinks,' he started. 'First, the station warrant officer tells me that the squadron airmen won't obey any orders except from their own officers and NCO's. You had better get this straightened out, but fast, or else someone's going to wind up in the glasshouse.' Then, turning to us: 'As for my officers, I can't find anything to like about you. You are the most conceited and insubordinate bunch of bastards it's ever been my misfortune to meet in my service career. You dress like bums, you steal airforce petrol for your cars, you drink like fishes, you don't sleep and you've made a night club out of your billet, where your girl friends spend the night.

'One of my flight commanders comes out of hospital on crutches, and puts on an exhibition with an officer from another squadron. I won't have him in my squadron.'

'It was a damned good exhibition,' I said, my hackles rising.

'I'll come to you later,' said Kent, giving me the full blast of his ice-cold eyes. 'I have two complaints in front of me from the police. One concerns a game-keeper who caught you poaching pheasants and the other, a speeding violation. Your Lincoln Mercury, Bartley. I notice most of you all drive high-powered automobiles which are neither licensed nor insured, but I understand you have made an arrangement with a local constable whereby he tips you off before they run a check. As for your dress – I can hardly call it uniform – I will not tolerate check shirts, old school ties, suede shoes nor red trousers. Your record in the air is undisputed, but it could have been much better, and without your appalling casualties, so you are going to smarten up, and fast. You may dismiss.'

We filed sullenly from the office. 'How about that?' said Wimpy, 'Do you think he'll really sack Brian?'

'Over my dead body,' I said. 'I'll ask for a posting.'

The WAAF officers were giving a party that night to which we were invited. I got hold of Bunty Hanbury, the senior WAAF, and told her in highly coloured terms what had happened, so that Kent could hear. I said I was going to ask for a posting to another squadron, in which case the others would follow. Bunty told me to cool it, and to go and find Paula whom she'd invited especially for me.

Later, when we were all good and high, Johnnie got me in a corner. 'You know you're a sloppy bunch of bums,' he said. 'But pretty decent ones at that, so help me straighten things out. I know I can't win without you and Brian on my side, and I didn't mean what I said about sacking him. So give me a break, will you?' He held out his hand and I shook it.

I found her in another room, where a station band was playing. Bob had taken over the piano, and she was standing behind him. Golden hair, and blue eyes like the sky at thirty thousand feet. I took her in my arms and we started to dance. She was soft and delicate as Dresden china. We didn't talk. Our thoughts, we kept to ourselves. During our time together, she never asked me about my fear, or about our future. She understood, and accepted things as they had to be. She knew only two things really counted with me, the squadron and the war. She had become mine, and when all the drink and postmortems were done, I would take her, and she would make me forget my fear in the love we shared.

By November, the Hun had started on different daylight tactics of fighter and fighter bomber 'sweeps' of Me 109s in formations of various sizes. Their bombs were dropped indiscriminately, and as soon as they saw our Spitfires coming for them.

Each side reached for maximum height and surprise attack from above and out of the sun when there was any. Thereafter, an air battle evolved into sections or individual dog fighting. The 'heavies' blasted away at London, by night.

On November 1st I shared a 109 with Bob Holland and French Sergeant Pilot de Montbron, a Count by birth, who'd decided to call himself French Canadian if taken prisoner, which he ultimately was, and got away with his disguise.

On November 5th I shot down another after 92 had been jumped from the sun. The pilot baled out and safe landed near Southend. The squadron maintained its code of not shooting parachuting ducks, as was followed by all Fighter Command. Nor did we shoot an enemy downed in the sea. In fact, we radioed his position to be picked up by whom it might best concern. On the occasion I went out in an air-sea rescue launch to pick up a pilot in his dinghy about five miles off Calais, a 109 circled us, and just waggled his wings, much to my great relief, but the Navy appeared unperturbed.

We could put our squadron team of officers and sergeant pilots into the air boasting a collection of seven decorated out of the twelve. The sergeant fighter pilots lived in their own sphere of companionship and recreation in off duty hours. An anomalous *modus vivendi* for a bunch of friends who fought together and protected each other's lives in the air, I used to think. Tradition at its worst. The pub they patronised was adjacent to the airfield, and called The Jail. Ours was the White Hart with its much loved owner and confidante to all fighter pilots, Cathy Preston.

The Few, as we became called after Churchill's famous speech, were a generation born to war, as a generation earlier our fathers were. Some of us were men, but most still boys. Some had an idea what it was all about, but most did not. We were fit and fearless, in the beginning. By the end, we were old and tired, and knew what fear was. I had taken a life before I had taken a woman. Both experiences I found bore similar emotions…apprehension,

The Blackout Board at The White Hart, Brasted

excitement, sensuality and a sense of great achievement. We expected to die, but, in the meantime were determined to live every minute of each day.

Aeroplanes were our first love, followed by girls and alcohol. All three were indispensable to our existence. Air combat was a personal, individual challenge, because we fought alone, man against man. A contest of gladiators in the vast arena of the sky. A deadly sport of flying and marksmanship.

We had no comrades marching shoulder to shoulder. No pipes or drums, and the loneliness was sometimes more frightening than the bullets. If one lost one's nerve, it was easy to run away. The sky is a big place to get lost in. But we didn't run.

The Few came from many parts of the world, and from every walk of life, which was the backbone of our strength. We complemented one another. What one lacked, the other made up for, so that the overall conglomerate was complete and indestructible. Most people in their lifetime have made one paramount endeavour, and I believe that with most airmen, this was in the war.

How did it leave us? Most I flew with went forward in their peacetime lives, but a number collapsed, exhausted athletes, never to regain their wind. What would we have been without our war experience? The fear, the wounds, the prison camps? Would we have ever reached the emotional heights, the lows, the broad horizons, the love, the trust, the brotherhood of man?

To have lived with death, places an indelible value on life.

The Battle of Britain had come to its inevitable and victorious end. The fighter pilots who had survived, retired to lick their wounds, and drink deeply of the fruits of their victory.

Christmas Day dawned black and overcast, and I dragged myself out of bed with a sore head from the previous night's celebration. There was a large barrel of beer in our dispersal hut, and the stove was red hot.

I wished my crew a Happy Christmas, and presented each of them with a bottle of sherry. We finished the barrel of beer by midday, and repaired to the airmen's mess to serve Christmas dinner to our men an air force custom since the days of the Royal Flying Corps in World War One. As the officers filed out of the kitchen, bearing triumphantly the plates of steaming turkey, they were greeted with cheers from their squadron members, more to attract attention to an empty place setting, than due to the individual popularity of the officer.

'92 Squadron over here, Sir,' our men chorused.

We returned to our Mess to eat our own Christmas fare thereafter and the sergeants called on us in late afternoon. The bar stayed open all day and through the night while we danced and celebrated until dawn.

*

In the first week of January, the squadron was moved down to Manston. The airfield had been evacuated during the Battle of

'Heroes of the Battle of Britain' (l. to r.) S/Ldr A C Bartley, DFC; W/Cdr F B Sheen, DFC; W/Cdr R Gleed, DSO; W/Cdr M Aitkin, DFC; W/Cdr A G Malan, DSO; S/Ldr A C Deere, DFC; Air Chief-Marshal Sir Hugh Dowding; F/Off. E C Henderson, MM; F/Lt R H Hilary, DFC; W/Cdr J H Kent, DFC; W/Cdr C B F Kingcome, DFC and S/L D H Watkins, DFC.

Britain, and it was still considered to be in the heart of the 'Indian' country. The Luftwaffe made a habit of using cloud cover from which to launch their bombing and machine gun attacks, intermittently.

Manston was a mess, and we felt we had been banished there in order to sever our connections with our notorious 92nd Night Club. The whole area had been evacuated, and turned into a forward defence zone. We were billeted in a drab requisitioned boarding house in Margate, the only building left standing in a bombed-out block. It had neither heat, light nor window glass. We spent one night there, with sporadic sleeping in our flying clothing, having generated sufficient warmth from a couple of bottles of whisky. The next morning, we walked out with no intention of ever returning.

Our duties were convoy patrols over the cruel sea, a more deadly enemy than the Me 109s. We were under continuous air attack, so rigged up an ingenious chute from the crew-room window into an adjacent air raid shelter down which we could slide at the sound of the air raid warning.

The first day we were released, we each went our separate ways to Canterbury, and there, with some embarrassment, found some of us in the Cathedral kneeling in prayer for our deliverance, before meeting up with the rest at our predetermined rendezvous of local repute to tie one on.

On January 10th the weather was clear and we were briefed to cover a bomber raid on a target in Calais harbour. We rendezvoused with six Blenheims close escorted by the Northolt Wing. We were to act top cover. The flak was intense over the target, but it was good to see our bomber boys pounding the enemy, for a change. We must have taken them by surprise, as none of their fighters came up to intercept. Our only hazard was an engine failure over the sea which in winter could inflict a cold, cruel, lingering death.

A week later, two sections of our team shot up a Ju 87 who had been attacking one of our ships, a fishing trawler off Ramsgate. The pilot knew that his only escape route was to force land on our airfield, and made a desperate attempt to do so. Sammy Saunders called off his section when he realised the scenario, but suddenly a Spitfire zeroed in, and shot the Junkers' wing off with a burst of cannon fire. We were horrified to see the enemy dive into the ground and burst into flames. Outraged that anyone could have shot a practically sitting bird. Not cricket. The culprit, a sergeant pilot, was less sympathetic. The Adjutant told us later that his wife and child had been killed in an air raid, the previous month.

Four of our Spitfires had been equipped with 20-millimetre cannons for trial purposes, and I was flying one of them. On 3rd February it was a cloudy morning when I was at readiness and ordered to scramble to intercept a lone bandit over the Thames estuary. It was luck that I saw his bombs explode below me on Hornchurch, and looking up, I spotted an He 111. The experiment was on.

I told the Controller the situation and that I was armed with cannon. I added that I'd leave my transmitter on and give a running commentary. As I got within range, the Heinkel's gunner started shooting at me and the aircraft started diving for the ground. Within range, I opened fire from dead astern. The cannons shook my plane, and I saw the shells exploding on his fuselage. His rear gunner stopped firing simultaneously, and the Heinkel started to disintegrate, tail first. A gout of blood splashed my windshield. Then bodies started to bale out, but no parachutes opened.

'The bugger's blown to pieces,' I yelled over the RT. The Heinkel plunged into the sea with a cascade of spray.

When I landed, the Controller was on the Ops phone to me. Fighter Command was delighted with the result of my cannons, but not my language. From this encounter and my simultaneous commentary of the results, I am of the opinion that the Air Ministry finally decided to adopt this armament as standard.

At the end of February, the squadron moved back to Biggin Hill,

and our return called for a succession of alcoholic celebrations. The
Station Commander, 'Mongoose' Soden would not allow us to
reoccupy our former billet, however, and we were moved into some
married quarters adjacent to the officers' mess which had been
vacated, and where he could keep his eye on us.

It had been decided to change fighter tactics for the new
offensive to be carried out over France and the Low Countries, and
the first to evolve was the formation of three squadrons into a wing,
Sailor Malan being promoted wing commander and Mungo-Park
taking over 74 which moved to Manston. Simultaneously, Johnnie
Kent was promoted to take over a wing at Northolt which once again
left us without a CO. We all had hopes that the appointment would
go to Brian Kingcome, but this wasn't to be, and a week later Jamie
Rankin walked into the officers' mess.

Johnnie Kent

Wimpy Wade and I were having a drink in the bar after the
day's action, when I spotted Jamie's entrance. With a 'long time no
see' I greeted him and asked him to join us in a drink which
grinning, he accepted.

I asked him what he was doing at Biggin, and how were things at
our old station Drem. Somewhat nervously, I thought, he answered
that he'd left Drem and been posted to Biggin to take over 92.

Wimpy and I almost choked over our pints, then Wimpy said,

'Well, then you just stick around and we'll teach you the form.' He finished his drink, and walked out of the bar.

'I apologise for that, Jamie. He's a rude bugger, a great fighter pilot and doesn't mean any harm,' I said.

'They warned me about you all at Fighter Command,' Jamie grinned. 'I was told your treatment of some of your late commanding officers has been pretty rough.'

'That's the way with us, I'm afraid,' I grinned back. 'But don't you worry about it. I'll talk to the boys and give you a great build-up. First, I'll introduce you to Brian Kingcome. If you can make time with him, you're in with the rest. I'll see to that.'

That evening, I took Jamie along to a party the MacNeal twins were giving at their house. Most of the boys were there, including Brian, and I introduced Jamie to all. Later, the Sailor got me in a corner and told me I was a goddam playboy, as were the rest of my tribe. That the only responsibility we ever showed was in the air, and then we were a better team than any, but notwithstanding, he was going to make me a proposition.

Brian Kingcome

'I propose to give you a flight in 74 if you promise to behave yourself on the ground. Think it over, and give me your answer first thing in the morning, when you've sobered up.'

I had never wanted to leave the squadron, but all around me my friends were leaving for promotion and added responsibilities, so the next morning, I reported to Sailor and told him I'd settle down and accept his offer with gratitude. I said my goodbyes to the boys, my flight sergeant mechanics, my fitters and riggers, armourers and Ops Clerk Webber. Then, I packed my bags and made my departure.

The take-over of the 92nd Night Club by 609, commanded by Mike Robinson, on their posting to Biggin somewhat mollified the sorrow of my decision to leave its ambience. His brother-in-law, Paul Richey, was a flight commander, and they made a glamorous pair of highly decorated fighter pilots who attracted equal glamour from the ranks of Mayfair society, the theatre and the Press. Guest evenings became pretty regular occurrences. Par for their course. One evening, the Oliviers and Noël Coward had put on a show in the only standing hangar to entertain the station officers and men. Thereafter, they were entertained in the officers' mess where Larry was accosted by a stage struck female guest at the party who asked him what was the proudest moment in his life.

'Was it when you married Vivien Leigh?' she cooed.

'No,' Larry replied. 'It is a memory of when I was once bowled out in a school cricket match by Douglas Bader.'

When I had accepted Sailor Malan's offer, I determined to stick to the bargain, and turn over a new leaf. First, I sold my Lincoln Zephyr so I had no longer any need to milk the petrol bowsers, and I started to dress like an RAF officer. However, I found that I had little in common with the pilots of 74 squadron, and that our squadron commander Mungo-Park was a tired, sick man and drinking heavily.

Gradually, I managed to win the confidence, even friendship of my flight, but few of them appeared to like each other. They were a real mixed-up bunch, the complete antithesis of 92. Mungo had an extraordinary obsession about the quality and capabilities of his pilots, and would disbelieve or discredit any account of a combat success that they claimed.

Our operations were confined to convoy patrols, weather permitting, and there were little signs of the enemy. Both sides were pretty well socked in. On April 6th I was briefed to go to an airfield behind St Omer, using low cloud cover, to shoot a group of young Luftwaffe pilots who Intelligence had told us were having their 'passing out' parade. I took a young New Zealand pilot with me, and neither of us relished the assignment. We had never before been involved in such brutality against the human race, and the thought revolted us, but those were our orders. I wondered why Mungo had selected me for this savage task. A strange malevolence, I had to think.

As we approached our target, I thought of their pride in their new wings, exactly as mine had been. As we swept over their parade ground, took aim and pressed the trigger of our eight machine guns, I nearly threw up.

On the way home, we were jumped by an Me 110 who had sneaked up behind us as we approached the coast. Neither of us had any thoughts other than those for the young airmen we had murdered. As a hail of lead whipped by our wing tips, both of us spontaneously looped into cloud cover, and upon emerging, found our attacker right in front of us, an easy target which we destroyed.

I landed at Hawkinge to check what damage I might have sustained, I told myself, but in truth I wanted time to regain my composure before facing my squadron again. When I had landed back at Manston, Mungo sent for me and asked what the hell I thought I was doing wasting time at Hawkinge.

'Seeing your friends, I suppose,' he snarled. He knew that Paddy Green and Bob Holland were now stationed there. 'You come straight back, in future. You won't behave in my squadron as you did in your bloody outfit,' he concluded.

I turned my back and walked out. Poor, gallant, basically nice Mungo, I then realised, had been broken by the war. He had become a paranoiac case.

On April 10th I found myself alone at thirty thousand feet when I spotted an Me 109 a few thousand feet below me, and dived almost vertically down to attack him. Suddenly, my eardrums exploded with awful pain, forcing me to pull out to try to clear my eustacian tubes, but failed. The 109 hadn't seen me, and I prayed that there was no other enemy around, as I could only spiral slowly back to earth to prevent my eardrums bursting, or the pain resulting in my losing consciousness. When I had touched down and started rolling to a halt, I fainted.

The doctors came to their quick diagnosis. Both my eardrums were cracked. A consultant to the RAF and the King's autologist, Sir Milson Rees, took over my case, and within three weeks he had it cured.

I was ordered on sick leave, and the autologist asked me, as compensation for his services, whether I would agree to subject myself to an experimentation on a pet theory of his that humans had a latent homing pigeon instinct in their inner ear which he would like to try and activate in mine. I told him I'd rather he tried this out on some other guinea-pig, and reported to a Medical Board, stating that I was now ready to return to Ops, but they ruled otherwise.

And thus, one whole year after my first operational sortie over

Dunkirk, I was posted out of Fighter Command.

Within a month, Mungo and three of my pilots were shot down and killed, and I thought to myself, but for the grace of God and my eustacian tubes, I would have also been.

I also thought of the savage world of our own. Gladiators in a sky arena, where we fight to the death, as our Roman forebears did, for reasons our governments had decreed, without animosity towards the enemy. The bombers, maybe, yes, but a German fighter pilot was no different from us, and I respected him as such. I wondered whether, when he returned to earth, the girls congregated around him in the sanctuary of some village, notwithstanding a conquered one, as they did in mine. With peace offerings of their femininity, part sexual, part maternal, part masochistic in making love to a young man who could be killed on the morrow. We accept their gratuity, but feel more secure in male chauvinistic companionship. Drinking with our tribe. After fighting at thirty thousand feet we made indifferent lovers. Our nights pre-empted by our dreams of the dreaded smoke trails in the sky.

CHAPTER SIX

Test Pilot

Janet heard from Paddy what had happened to me and invited me down to her country house, Tracadie, to recuperate. I had told Paddy that I never wanted to see another aeroplane again, and he had asked Janie to sort me out.

I slept twelve hours a day, started to eat again, lazed in the Spring sunshine and listened to the songs of the birds. For the first time since Dunkirk I was at peace with the world, except that Paula and I had had a lovers' quarrel, and she had incarcerated herself in London with her work. So be it, par for the course, I made myself think. I wasn't going to risk a bomb in London. I'd had enough where I'd come from.

Towards the end of my leave, my posting came through to an Operational Training Unit at Sutton Bridge in Lincolnshire to where I made my lonely pilgrimage. The commanding officer was a permanent commissioned officer who had little time for the riffraff, as he referred to us young irregular war volunteers, and he warned us to watch our manners and behaviour if we wanted to live in an officers' mess.

I had lost my second stripe, because there was no establishment for another flight lieutenant on the OTU and somehow, the word got back to the C in C of Eleven Group, Trafford Leigh-Mallory, and he sent for me. I told him I was miscast in Training Command and requested a posting back to a squadron. This, he refused, but had me transferred to another OTU at Heston, where he knew already incumbent were some of my friends, Bob Holland, Brian Kingcome, John Bisdee, Tiny Kinder and Ronnie Fokes. And there, I also met up with Humphrey Gilbert for the first time who was to become as good a friend as I ever had, and for whose death I was to become, in part, responsible for.

Humphrey was test flying a twin-engined night fighter fitted with radar and a powerful searchlight in its nose. It was classified top secret, and he didn't talk about it. He was the biggest playboy of us all, and had a Ministry car and small communications plane at his disposal, and with Bob Holland and myself became the third musketeer in our carousing and London night clubbing. However, as a flying instructor, I proved a dismal failure. The life just wasn't mine, and one day I flew over to Biggin Hill to tell my troubles to the Sailor.

Visiting him, at the time, was Jeffrey Quill, a friend of his and chief test pilot (experimental) of Vickers Supermarine Aircraft Company, makers of the Spitfire, and his visit was not merely a social one. He was looking for a Spitfire pilot with combat experience to recruit for his test team on loan from the RAF. Sailor looked at me and grinned over his tankard of beer, having made the introduction. I nodded my head with excitement, and ordered another round.

'I could recommend this one, if you keep him on a tight rein,' the Sailor grinned once more. Jeffrey studied me for a moment, and then held out his hand. I took it, and the deal was made, when Sailor had made a quick call to the Head of Personnel at Fighter Command who had fixed our band for the 92nd Night Club.

I was installed at the Polygon Hotel in Southampton in the third week of July, and introduced to my co-pilots George Pickering, George Lowdel, George Sneary and Geoffrey Wedgewood, also seconded from the RAF.

George Lowdel

My duties were devoted to the production test line, and when each new aircraft had been wheeled out of the factory and engine tested, we flew it off the ground for its virgin flight, with a pad strapped to one knee upon which to note engine performance figures, speeds and general handling at various altitudes up to twenty thousand feet. The descent was made in a terminal velocity test dive and pull out at over five hundred miles per hour to see that the wings didn't come off, and generally give the new aircraft a good stretch. It was invariably found that on climb it would fly one wing low, and sometimes require considerable force on the stick to keep it in horizontal plane, and after the TV dive it would be inclined to the other. On landing adjustments were made to the trimming tabs on both wings and tail plane, and the aeroplane subsequently tested until it would fly straight and level, hands and feet off the controls.

My whole life became absorbed in test flying the only aircraft I had ever wanted to fly, and my evenings spent drinking with my new test pilot friends, mostly in George Pickering's Clausentum Club in Southampton. Some weekends I would take one of our communication planes, and fly up to Hendon to carouse with my old chums, or to Shoreham where Janie would collect me in her car to take me to her home at Henfield. At others, I would visit Biggin Hill to drink with Sailor and Jamie Rankin who was proving a popular CO and fighter ace of the top rank. I saw a lot of new faces, few of the old and felt somewhat of a stranger, but the nostalgia was there.

All my expenses were paid, and I bought myself a motor car, as my other perks included an unlimited supply of petrol. For a while, I thought I had it made.

One evening, late, I was collecting my key from the front desk, when I bumped into Noël Coward whom I'd met at the Biggin Hill camp concert. He told me that he was on a film location in Southampton (*In Which We Serve*) and deplored the fact that the bar was closed. I told him I had a bottle of whisky in my room to which we promptly adjourned to broach it. I wanted to call Paula but didn't have a room phone, so telling Noel to get on with the booze, I returned to the lobby to use the kiosk. When I got back to my room, Noel was lying on my bed in a silk dressing-gown, whisky in hand.

'Thought I'd make myself comfortable, dear fellow,' said he.

'Going to make a pass at any moment,' thought I, preparing to throw him out on his ass. We talked of my war, his film, and finished the bottle. Then he said goodnight and left, and I'll never know!

It was a strange and lonely life compared to the communal existence of a squadron, and whenever I could get a break I would fly up to Heston, and join up with Bob, and Humphrey in London. During the next six months I learned as much about the Spitfire and how to fly it, as anyone. I also learned what a great job the men in the factory, which was a target for bombers, were doing.

Part of the Fighter Command philosophy behind seconding

George Sneary

fighter pilots as test pilots to the aircraft manufacturers was to advise the designers of required improvements based on combat experience.

The original Rolls Royce engine had been substantially increased in power and weight, but still contained within the same airframe. This had the effect of creating instability in a very tight turn in which the aircraft could get locked, imposing centrifugal forces which not only blacked out the pilot but could pull off the wings. I told the company test pilots about this phenomenon, who checked it out and got their designers to work on it. I also believed, from personal experiences, that it was a rare occasion when one saw the enemy that shot one down on account of the blind area behind the pilot, due to the basic aircraft design. To eliminate this would entail a radical redesign, a sketch of which I drew for the manufacturers. Basically, this consisted of lowering the height of the fuselage behind the cockpit, and substituting a balloon canopy in place of the original. This was agreed to by the designers, and incorporated in the subsequent models of the Spitfire. The American Mustang P 51 followed this design.

Although the design and production centres of the Spitfire were in the proximity of Southampton, the assembly of the components was mostly undertaken in areas dispersed from the bombers' target, on the orders of Lord Beaverbrook, Janie's father and Minister of Aircraft Production. The nearest one was Worthydown, a Fleet Air Arm aircrew training base outside Winchester. Others were at Chattis Hill and High Post further afield, and in fact were only fields large enough to fly in and out a Spitfire, and erect prefabricated hangars for assembly.

To reach these, the test pilots flew out of East Leigh, our base, through a small gap between the cables of the barrage balloon cables which we couldn't see but judged its path by following the railway line to Winchester. We used our fleet of small communication planes. If the motor cut on take off, there was no turning back, and it was even more precarious flying in, as there was no going around again in the event of a misjudged approach. In a light plane one could handle it, but not in a Spitfire.

Larry Olivier, now a lieutenant in the Fleet Air Arm, was stationed at Worthydown flying trainee wireless operators around in Proctors, a soul-destroying job, he told me, from which he had made an unsuccessful attempt, on account of his age, to transfer to Ops. He and Vivien had a cottage nearby, and transported themselves on a motor bike as this was all their petrol ration would allow.

Others luminaries of stage and screen would visit them sporadically and I joined in parties in the officers' mess and the Olivier home. Thus started a very long friendship which I treasured. Ralph Richardson and Roger Livesey had both previously done a little solo flying, and begged me to give them a refresher course of dual instruction sufficient to get them in good enough shape to help qualify for their applications to join the RAF as pilots. I had to tell them that, due to their age, and lack of sufficient flying hours, my contribution wouldn't help their aspirations.

Leslie Howard was making a propaganda film to immortalise R.J. Mitchell, the designer of the Spitfire, and I was invited with Jeffrey Quill to do the aerobatics. Leslie wanted to capture the authentic atmosphere of a fighter station, and I took him over to Biggin. Sailor Malan was back commanding the station, and I was apprehensive as to how he would react to visiting movie stars. He had just landed from a fighter sweep when we arrived, and had blood of a tail gunner splashed over his windscreen, so he was quite hospitable.

When Leslie and his writers had seen what they wanted, it was suggested that the film could benefit by some authentic characters, so an arrangement was made with Fighter Command to lend some fighter pilots, including myself, to Leslie Howard Productions. We were put up at the Savoy Hotel, in the custody of the publicity controller, who was responsible for delivering us to Denham Studios every morning. I don't know whether we succeeded in contributing authenticity, but we spent a couple of thousand pounds in entertaining ourselves at the company's expense.

On October 14th, Humphrey had flown to Worthydown a light plane to pick me up for a party of his in London. We had a few drinks with Larry and Vivien in the Ladies Room of the Officers' Mess after which we repaired to the aircraft but found that we couldn't start the motor owing to some mechanical failure. We looked at one another and then simultaneously at the Spitfire I had just finished testing. There was only one alternative. We had to make the party. Humphrey got in, and I sat on his lap. We couldn't use straps, or close the hood. Neither could one of us handle all the controls. I took the stick, the throttle and right rudder, Humphrey the left, the pitch and the undercarriage lever. We opened up and staggered into the air. Immediately, we realised that we were in dead trouble, and I tried to get my left foot onto the other pedal. In the attempt, I kicked the stick forward which bucked the aircraft and shot me outwards. Humphrey grabbed, and hauled me back into the cockpit. We decided we'd have to let things be. When we got to Heston, we both knew there could be no 'going round again'. We motored in, and made a passable landing. I jumped out and Humphrey taxied in. When he had switched off, we solemnly swore that we would never try tandem again.

We had hardly ordered our first drink when an apoplectic Station Commander attacked us. 'What in the hell do you think you're doing?' he bellowed. 'I'll have you court-martialled for this.'

It transpired that the stupefied flying control, when asked the name of the pilot, had replied: 'There were two, Sir.' Fortunately, the Station Commander was a veteran of the last war, and six double gins later, we were forgiven, but banned from ever landing at Heston again.

During November, I got an urgent call from Gordon Brettel. He was being court-martialled for flying a WAAF on his lap to a dance in a Spitfire. One of the three charges was endangering the King's aircraft, for which he could expect a severe penalty. He asked me if I would testify in his defence. I said I would, and to expect me at Biggin where he was stationed with 92 Squadron.

I explained my friend's predicament to Jeffrey Quill and Joe Smith, our chief designer at Supermarines, and Joe agreed to write me out some mathematical equations relating to centres of gravity which no one would understand and which would prove irrefutably that the King's aircraft was never in any danger, subject to knowing the size of the young lady. I was able to give this from personal experience, that her dimensions, although substantial, would not interfere with the controls of the aircraft.

I produced this evidence at the court-martial and the prosecuting counsel asked how I could prove it. 'I've done it', I said, 'and if the Court so pleases, I'd be happy to fly prosecuting counsel on my lap.' The court hastily recessed – counsel declined, and Gordon Brettel was acquitted on that charge.

Despite all the activity, my relative freedom of action, my petrol allowance and the new friends I had made, I missed the camaraderie and ambience of a fighter station to which I knew I really belonged. Test flying was exciting, a challenge, and could prove hazardous. George Pickering's wings flew off in a terminal velocity dive which almost cost him his life. But I had learned to fly a Spitfire as well as anyone or better, except that my mentor Jeffrey Quill, which was to stand me in invaluable stead, and probably saved my life on my many operational actions I knew I was, in the future to encounter.

I was suddenly transferred to the Castle Bromwich factory when their chief test pilot* went down with appendicitis, and was billeted with the managing director, Richard Dixon, and his wife, in a requisitioned manor house, who came to treat me as a son. I flew in appalling Midlands' weather, harder than I'd ever flown. My engine cut out over a built-up area, but against cardinal air rules, I turned back, missing a hangar roof by a hair's-breadth. I seldom visited London any more. I felt desperately alone.

It was in February 1942 when my loneliness, my remoteness and my conscience dictated that I should return to war, as my other friends had done. Humphrey Gilbert was commanding 65 Fighter Squadron at Debden, and by the strings I had now learned to pull and, indeed, thought I was entitled to, I was posted to join him as his flight commander. Johnnie Peel, who commanded the Station, was a close friend of Max and Janet Aitken which smoothed my flight path.

I bade farewell to the test pilots, and the friends I had made on the factory floor and headed northwards in my Hudson Terraplane.

It had been an eye-opener and of great interest to witness the production element of this war effort towards a mutual goal, and I

* Alex Henshaw.

had made many friends amongst the men and women who contributed in this aim.

Someone was reputed to have said that it was easier for a child and a fighter pilot to make friends with strangers than anyone else, and I believe this was true. Some pilots never grew up. The craftsmen who built our machines took great pride in their work, and liked to befriend the young gladiators who flew them.

CHAPTER SEVEN

The Second Round

Sixty-five Squadron had been re-assigned to a night fighter role, but Humphrey had assured me before I joined that this couldn't last, and I knew from my experience at Pembrey, that he would be proved right. A Spitfire could never make a night fighter. However, we gave it a whirl according to a crazy new *modus operandi* in which we circled a vertical searchlight beam on standing patrols, and when an enemy bomber came within range, another beam would point us in its direction. Our aircraft were painted jet black as the night, and were completely without success. Not long after we reverted to our proper function and started operating as a Wing on offensive sweeps and bomber escorts.

In the middle of March Geoff Wellum joined the squadron as a flight commander, and it was a happy reunion for both of us. April brought fine weather by which time Humphrey had welded a fine team together, and the battle was once more on.

In the first week on an air sea rescue mission, we were bounced in mid channel by a bunch of FW 190s which outclassed our Mark 5b Spits. It developed into one hell of a dog-fight, but oddly enough neither side suffered casualties.

It was during this struggle that I experienced, again, the danger of the instability of the Mark 5b in a very tight turn. It tightened up on itself to a degree where it was difficult to get out – exactly what I had begun to suspect when testing the new type at Supermarines.

Geoffrey Wellum

The end result of this startling aerodynamic development, I realised, could only end sooner or later in disaster.

On mentioning this to Johnnie Peel in the Mess that evening, he told me he had just had encountered the same experience in pulling out of a steep dive. The involuntary 'g' forces this had imposed had blacked him out, and bashed his head against the gun sight. I told him I'd get on to Jeffrey Quill and have him fly up, soonest, to ascertain the cause of this lethal problem. The next day, he did, and flew one of our squadron aircraft back to Southampton to test and ascertain the cause of this very dangerous development.

One day, a communications plane that had engine trouble landed, and out of it stepped a beautiful female ferry pilot. Her name was Diana Barnato, and she was the granddaughter of the famous 'Barney' who had once owned most of the Kimberly diamond mine. Her father had been a famous motor racing driver and one time international playboy, now Wing Commander Admin in the RAF Reserve. I had first met her at a Stowe school dance, when I was sixteen. She subsequently became the first woman to fly more than one thousand miles per hour.

I introduced her to Humphrey whose eyes lit up like two of her grandfather's diamonds, and he invited her to have a drink with us in the officers' mess, which she accepted. While thus engaged, Humphrey got me aside and said, 'Fix her aeroplane, pronto', whereupon I excused myself and went out to the hangar outside which the aeroplane was parked and where my flight sergeant had told me that he had fixed the problem, so, I told him to unfix it. CO's orders.

He just gave me a very broad wink, and answered, 'Aye, Aye, Sir.'

It took four days to find out what had been wrong with Diana's aeroplane, during which time she and Humphrey became inseparable.

Jeffrey Quill called to tell me that they had discovered what had been causing the Mark 5's instability in a tight turn, and that modification orders were being sent to all Spitfire squadrons. In confidence, he added that over twenty unaccountable accidents had been recorded, and that the suspicion had been on wing failure due to excessive 'g' in combat. He added that he reckoned I'd saved a great many more casualties, and I realised that my attachment as a test pilot to Supermarines had more than justified itself.

I settled down with confidence to our new offensive warfare over northern Europe, mounting fighter sweeps and bomber escort as a

Jeffrey Quill

wing of Spitfires. The two other squadrons were the famous 71st Eagle and 111 Squadron which I was to command on my third tour of Ops in North Africa. We were naturally compatible types, so it seemed, became close friends and made up an indomitable team.

Pete Peterson, the first American ace, commanded the Eagle squadron, and we used to chuckle at their wisecracks over the RT in the thick of battle which gave us added fortitude.

'Say, Oscar. They're 109s out back. Ain't yer goin' ter turn?'

In mid-April the squadron moved to the satellite airfield of Great Samford where we developed into a rather tight-knit community being segregated from the rest of the wing, except in the air. There, we were employed almost continuously on fighter sweeps and bomber escorts, rendezvousing with the Debden squadrons in the air. My log book recorded the bombers' targets as St Omer, Hazebrouck, Gravelines, Andrieuc, Le Touquet, Calais, Dunkirk, Abbeville, Ostend, Cap Gris Nez, Flushing, Ypres and Zeebrugge.

The FW 190s gave us a lot of trouble which came to a climax on April 27th over St Omer, where we were escort cover to a squadron of Bostons, which can best be described by a letter Geoff Wellum wrote me after the war.

As the circus turned for home after the bombing, we were on the outside of the turn and got well and truly bounced by about forty 190s.

FO Davies and PO Grantham collided after the first attack, and Freddie Haslett was shot out of the sky. I had seen it coming, and tried to warn him on the RT, but to no avail. I couldn't help, as I was being truly clobbered by another 109. It all happened so quickly. The sight of Haslett and my own predicament still haunts me to this day. I just managed to make it back to Manston. You and Tommy Burke fought your way out via Calais, he told me, right on the deck, and you saved his life by shooting a Focke Wulf off his tail.

May 1st, 1942

At thirty thousand feet over Lille, we were jumped by a group of FW 190s. As Humphrey's number two was shot, he must have cut off all power and the following aircraft crashed into him. I watched the tangled, disintegrating mass go hurtling earthwards before I turned my section into our attackers. I called to the wing leader that we were in trouble, but I guess he had troubles of his own, since he didn't turn back. My section was on its own.

The next twenty minutes was the toughest I had ever had, and I squirmed and turned until I was down to sea level with my relentless opponents sniping at me in turns. I could see their cannon shells ploughing into the water around my shadow and I felt that this just had to be 'it', when one of them overshot and pulled right up in front of me. I hauled back on the stick and hanging on my prop, gave him a burst which spun him into the sea. Whether this discouraged his confederates I will never know, but all of a sudden I was alone.

I ploughed my aeroplane into the airfield at Biggin with a shattered undercarriage and asked flying control to pick up the pieces while I got myself a drink in the Mess. I telephoned Humphrey to give my status report and he told me we had lost four, and not to hurry back as the squadron was released for 48 hours, to lick our wounds.

May 2nd

As I flew into Debden I saw a Spitfire piled up just off the perimeter of the airfield. When I landed my flight sergeant met me with an ashen face. 'The CO's dead,' he said. 'They were drunk, Sir, and I tried to stop them. I took away the starter trolley, but they started on the batteries. I did everything I could to stop them, Sir.'

'Them, who's them?' I shouted.

'The CO had the Controller* on his lap. He said he had done it before. They were going to a party. 'Johnnie Peel pulled up in his car.

'I want to see him,' I said. We drove over to Humphrey's Spitfire and I watched them pick the crushed bodies from the debris. Then Johnnie took me away.

I sobered up the day of the funeral, so that I could talk to Humphrey's parents and tell them the lie we had concocted: 'They were in the squadron communications plane. Routine flight. Cause of accident unknown.' Even Diana believed it. When it was over, Max†, who had flown up for the funeral, put his arm around me, and said: 'Bolshie, you've got to get out of here. You're coming with me. Father's just back from America.' We flew down to Cherkley and landed in the garden. The Beaver was furious and told Max to fly the aircraft out. He and I held on the tail while Max revved up the motor to gather the impetus to lift the aircraft over the trees. Janie had driven up from Tracadie to spend the night with her father and take me back to her home the following day, for my forty-eight hours leave. But we were faced with an almost insurmountable dilemma Janie was practically out of petrol, and completely out of coupons, so there could be only one solution. We drove her car clandestinely up to the home farm where there was an idle tractor, and armed with an empty can and rubber tube I was merrily syphoning out the tractor's petrol when we were startled by a roar from the Beaver:

'What the hell do you think you're doing?'

It needed no explanation, so I just put the filled can in the back of Janie's car. 'Haven't you got your own petrol without having to steal mine?' the Beaver growled.

'No, Sir – we use up all we get just going to the local pubs and cinemas in our spare time,' I said.

'What do you do when you get any leave?' he asked, now gently.

'We have to thumb a ride from a car or a lorry, but it takes up most of our leave time,' I lied.

'This is an outrage,' roared the Beaver. 'Come with me.'

Janie and I accompanied our captor in silence back to his mansion wondering what punishment was in store for us. The Beaver picked up one of his telephones, and barked: 'Get Sir Archibald Sinclair.'

* Bill Ross † Max Aitken

'Christ,' I thought, 'I'm going to be reported to the Air Minister and court-martialled.' I listened to the conversation.

'Sinclair, Beaverbrook here. Do you know that when our fighter pilots get forty-eight hours leave they have to thumb rides in lorries to their homes because they haven't enough petrol for their cars?...No, I thought you didn't. I'd like to see an increase in their petrol allowances so they stop stealing mine!'

When I arrived back at Debden, Johnnie Peel told me that I'd got the squadron. Over my best friend's dead body, I had reached the height of my ambition – to command a fighter squadron.

We moved out to a satellite airfield of Debden's where we were on our own. I tried to run the squadron exactly as Humphrey had, but my flame had gone out. I went to London and Tracadie no more. I rented a cottage on the edge of the airfield and asked Paula to come and look after me. I hadn't seen much of her in the last six months, as Humphrey and I had made other female interests. But without hesitation or question, she agreed. I hated the long sweeps over the North Sea into enemy territory and found myself listening to every beat of my motor and watching my instruments for the dreaded sign of engine failure.

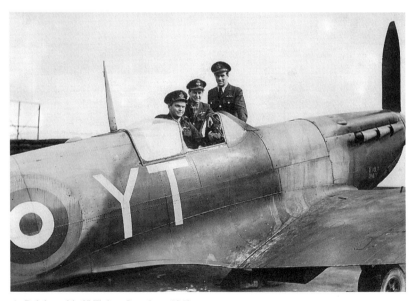

At Debden with 65 Fighter Squadron, 1942

From our dream house, Paula would watch us take off on our missions, count the planes out, and count them on their return. It became the only haven of peace I wanted now to return to, beat and exhausted, to find her there, waiting for me, looking as pretty and as fresh as a Spring flower. I could read the suffering in her face. I loved her with an almost savage possessiveness, and was terrified of losing her, because I had already lost so many I had loved.

Colin Hewlett joined the squadron to take over my flight, and our other replacements were Czech sergeant pilots straight from their OTUs. Fine young men and keen, but their casualties were inevitable, however hard I tried to nurse and protect them. I was awarded my Czech Wings which I wore with pride. The other two squadrons at Debden had also suffered many losses, including the Wing Commander, Pete Gordon, whose replacement was Duke Woolley.

We continued to sweep and escort the bombers and on the last day in May we swept the North Sea in search of any survivors of the 1000 bomber raid on Cologne, spotted some in dinghies, others without, and radioed their locations.

June was a repetition of the previous month. Towards the end we were assigned to practise deck landings on a marked out runway at Debden. What next undertaking we were in for, I hesitated to contemplate. Concisely, Geoff Wellum summed it up in another post war letter to me.

> Every day, almost, we were over Northern France, Belgium, Holland. My log book tells me Flushing, Abbeville, Lens, Béthune, Zeebrugge, Hazebrouck.
>
> My goodness, Tony, did we really do all that? And then, the Debden Wing was rumoured for Russia.

I was getting very tired, lost so many friends that sudden death had started to lose its threat, but the cruel sea and thoughts of imprisonment brought me out in a cold sweat, and my nightmares were becoming more frequent and more terrifying.

Johnnie Peel was beginning to suspect my condition. It was part of his job to learn his squadron commanders' feelings, as it was mine to know my pilots'. At the end of July, John told me I was being posted for a rest. I fought against it, but he was adamant.

I was posted to the school of air gunnery at Sutton Bridge which Sailor Malan was running, and he polished up my

65 Squadron pilots

marksmanship. When I had completed the course, I went on leave and thought about what I should do next. I also thought about my imprisoned friends Bob Tuck, Pete Casanove and Roger. I prayed that next time I would fight only within escape reach of friendly soil, in case I were shot down.

However, the mind works in mysterious ways. A young and healthy body is capable of complete rehabilitation. My leave had restored my strength in both. Rearmed and refuelled, I was ready to take on any challenge once more. I'd even forgotten the cruel sea.

A 'Think Tank' had figured that a great way, they thought, to shoot down the long-range German bombers (Condors) attacking our convoys to Russia. This was to equip merchant ships with an undercarriage-less Hurricane which could be catapulted off the deck, and take the attacker by surprise. Having disposed of his enemy down, the pilot would thereafter bale out in front of his parent ship, and pray that he would be retrieved before he froze to death.

Fortunately, Johnnie Peel who had been moved to the Air Ministry, had the recruitment for this action as part of his new duties, and after I had submitted my application, he put it at the very bottom of his pending file, and kept it there until I had got another posting.

This was to take over command of 111 Fighter Squadron now moved to Kenley, and destined for transfer overseas. Batchy

Atcherley was commanding the station and Brian Kingcome the Wing. Before the war, Batchy had electrified the spectators at an international air display in America. When the other stars had completed their aerobatic performances in souped-up monoplanes, Batchy, representing the Royal Air Force, and dressed in hunting pink with top hat, suddenly appeared astride a saddle strapped to the fuselage of a very old bi-plane which he was flying with reins. The aeroplane had landing wheels attached to its top-side, as well as underneath; he emulated every aerobatic manoeuvre the others had, then made a perfect upside down landing and thus stole the show.

He had an identical twin brother and both had applied to join the RAF together. One was slightly short on eyesight, the other on hearing, so, the good-sighted twin took and passed the eyesight tests for both, and his sharp-eared brother both their aural tests. The doctors never noticing the switch.

Batchy briefed me that the squadron had got run down and needed revitalising with fresh blood added to the team. I was to choose it and then bring it up to scratch before our overseas assignment which was not divulged. I picked Jimmy Baraldi and Mac Gilmour as my flight commanders. Jimmy was a few years older than me and a qualified chartered accountant. Mac, a Scot from the Highlands.

The huge ex-policeman: Sergeant Tommy Tinsey, who had flown as my number two in 65, was transferred at his request and at mine, and got him his commission as pilot officer.

When I had got them into flying shape as a team, I started on their air gunnery training at the ranges on the Isle of Sheppey in the Thames Estuary. I guessed we were destined for some army support action which entailed a lot of ground strafing which Sheppey specialised in.

Having flown my Spitfire to the adjacent airfield, made my arrangements with the gunnery officer, I then retired to the local RAF officers' mess, which I took for granted would provide a convivial luncheon session. I was 'battle dressed' and only identifiable by my squadron leader stripes. My reception was arctic. Nobody offered me a drink, so I treated myself. When I entered the dining-room, I saw the top table almost filled with senior officers. The rest of the tables were occupied by unhappy looking juniors. Naturally, I headed for the top table and was about to sit down, when a fat squadron leader (Admin) told me there was no place for me, and to sit with the junior officers.

'Screw you,' I said seating myself in an empty chair. 'I'm a senior officer.'

'Who's been sent here as a moral fibre case,' he sneered, 'which does not entitle you to sit at the Staff table.'

'Who the hell do you think you are talking to?' I said. 'I'm the Commanding Officer of 111 Fighter Squadron and I'm setting up an air to ground firing exercise on the gunnery range, and you'd better watch your lip or I'll use you for target practice.'

The Station Commander who had overheard this exchange, hurriedly left his chair, and came over and apologised to me. He told me that the station was a 'lack of moral fibre' trial centre. I took a pint of beer off him, and thought, 'Poor kids, it can happen to any of us.

When I had really got the boys in shape, I felt it was time for the blooding of their guns, and asked Batchy for the opportunity.

The first American Fighter Group had arrived in England and it was arranged that our wing commanded by Brian Kingcome would lead them on their first operational sortie. This was to be a shallow sweep over the Channel Ports of France.

I had Tommy Tinsey fly my number two, as he had in 65 Squadron, but now as a pilot officer. He joked that I had only arranged his transfer so that he would always fly behind me, to intercept with his huge frame any bullets aimed in my direction.

As the flak flew up at us, Brian gave a 'James Fitzpatrick' travelogue narration over the RT, and on turning homewards, concluded, 'And now we bid au-revoir to Le Touquet, once playground of the beautiful people, where the gaming tables are now empty, and the roulette wheels idle, waiting for the rest of you cowboys to come on over and help us finish the f… war.'

October 18th, 1942

Paula accompanied my father to see us off at Waterloo Station. I had all the squadron pilots with me. Hand-picked and keen. I had trained them how I wanted them. I was proud of them as I made the introductions. 'Boys, meet my father, Sir Charles Bartley. Tommy Tinsey, Jimmy Baraldi, Bill Draper,' and down the line of them. I was proud of my father too. He had recently retired from his long and distinguished service to India in its judiciary, and prime moved with other relatives and friends sufficient funds to pay for a squadron of Spitfires. Emblazoned upon their fuselages was the title

'92 East India Squadron'.

As the train pulled slowly out of the smoky station, I watched and waved to them from my carriage window. Two, suddenly, bereft people who loved me deeply in their own ways, and wondered if they would ever see me again, I knew.

CHAPTER EIGHT

Operation Torch

October 20th, 1942

The pilots were driven at dawn, from our northern transit camp to a canal near the Clyde. After an hour of waiting, a ten thousand ton freighter emerged from the mist, and we were shipped aboard. Our Spitfires were crated in two parts, wings and fuselages separate, to be put together at our point of debarkation. Our bunks had been crudely constructed in the centre hold. The only personal effects we had with us, were stowed in our parachute bags. We joined up with a huge convoy off Ireland, and headed south. Only the Commodore of the convoy knew our destination.

October 25th

The chief engineer was a Scot and we soon made friends. He told us the ship was carrying NAAFI stores in the forward hold which included cases of whisky and gin. He also told us about a catwalk which led from our accommodation to this treasure trove. A sliding panel was engineered and we took it in turns to crawl half the length of the ship, guided by flashlights and armed with our parachute bags to retrieve the booty. The Captain became suspicious since the Ward Room was strictly rationed, and our conduct not that sober. I suggested that the boys came well supplied for a long sea voyage, but when he saw the quantity of empties going overboard, he didn't believe it, but couldn't figure out how we were getting at his cargo.

October 30th

Speculation was rife, as the giant convoy suddenly swung towards the East, and the pilot boys were laying bets on our final destination. We had been conscripted to take a turn at 'duty watch', and on mine, I had sneaked into the chart room and seen our last position plotted due west of Gibraltar, so that meant the Mediterranean and not the Far East, as I had feared. An alternative, Malta or Alexandria, and I didn't look forward to the Malta run, which everybody knew was brutal.

November 4th

We sighted the coasts of Spain and Spanish Morocco simultaneously as we sailed into the narrows at dawn. The first sight of foreign shores for some.

'There's the Rock on the port bow', the skipper chuckled. 'Take a good look at it, as you won't be seeing another piece of British soil in quite a time, I reckon.' Pretty callous fellows, these seadogs, I thought, but wondered what they really thought. The whole voyage had been somewhat of a nightmare to most of us, unaccustomed to the seas, expecting to be torpedoed in our sleep, or suddenly see the *Scharnhorst* appear over the horizon. But now, we were on our last lap, while they, for the duration of the war would traverse the cruel seas infested with predators, on the surface or submerged. Carrying their lethal cargoes of gasoline and high explosives which hit by either bomb, shell or torpedo would send them all to kingdom come.

As the head of the convoy passed the Rock, my reflections were interrupted by a light flashing a signal at us from the Commodore's lead ship, then a line of flags were hoisted up its mast.

'It's Gib for you boys, and you can thank your lucky stars,' the skipper said. He had now been authorised to open his secret orders, and had read in them of Operation Torch, the Allied landings in North Africa. As our ship swung out of the convoy line, a row of bunting sprung from the masthead, spelling out an acknowledgement of the Commodore's signal, wishing him, 'Good luck, and God speed.'

Aldis lamps flashed from the Admiralty control tower as the SS *Hopecrown* slid into the bay. A pilot launch pulled up alongside, and a Commander RN climbed aboard. No sooner had the anchors secured the ship than an embarkation officer followed, and told us we had half an hour to pack our kit in preparation to disembark.

It was getting dark as we climbed down a rope ladder into a 'lighter' alongside, and as we pulled away, the crew of the *Hopecrown* lined the ship's side to give us a farewell send off. 'Good luck, boys', they shouted, and we chorused back, 'Goodbye and good luck, *Hopecrown*. Thanks for the ride'.

However, it transpired that we were not yet due to set foot on terra firma, and we were embarked on a nearby troopship which was loaded to the plimsoll line with American pilots and Rangers.

Having been conducted to a four berth cabin, which I was to share with three of my pilots, and dumped my kit, I made my way to the boat deck to stretch my legs.

The Rock was a blaze of lights, and the muffled roar simulating an industrial city, punctuated at intervals by the explosions of blasting operations, was carried across the bay on a subtropical breeze. I stood there, completely spellbound for several minutes marvelling at this beehive of activity...this fairyland of twinkling lights. Across the other side of the bay, the little whitewashed town of Algeciras nestled against the Spanish hills, reflecting pinpoints of yellow light which danced across the ruffled water.

I shook myself out of my reverie, realising that I was cold and hungry, and that I needed a very strong drink, so I made my way down to the crowded saloon. There, I was greeted by a heterogeneous crowd of servicemen, a cacophony of sound and an atmosphere of cigarette smoke. British and American officers were lounging in chairs playing cards or at the bar refuelling their glasses and shooting the breeze, the green grey of the American uniforms mingling with the khaki and Air Force blue of the British and Commonwealth. One could feel the tension and excitement everywhere. Through the crowd, I caught glimpses of a Dunkirk veteran, and a Battle of Britain pilot with the purple and white striped decoration under his wings.

I was standing in the doorway, trying to relate myself to the environment, when a large hand clamped down on my shoulder and an American voice drawled in my ear. 'Why, if it ain't Tony baby, for Chrissakes', and before I could put a name to it, a large whisky was thrust in my hand, and I placed the commander of a fighter squadron in the American Eighth with whom I had flown from Kenley. And so, another party got under way.

The Rangers left us on the evening of the second day with their marching orders. They just seemed to disappear into the night, and we knew that our turn wasn't many hours away. That zero hour was approaching.

When it came, and we had been ferried ashore, there was a lorry waiting for us at the quayside into which we piled ourselves and our baggage, contained in a parachute bag. No questions asked, no information offered. The lorry raced off, the driver banging his palm on the door panel to warn pedestrians of our approach. Motor horns were forbidden for some reason we were never given.

It followed a winding road almost to the summit of the Rock
where it deposited us outside the entrance of a transit camp. Rows of
Nissen huts stood inside, and the NCO in charge told us to take our
pick. Within, were iron beds, well worn mattresses and army
blankets. Our campaign initiation.

The rain started in torrents, and found its way through the seams
of the corrugated roofing making pools on the concrete floor. After
I'd dumped my kit, the NCO gave me directions to the officers' mess.

This, I discovered to be the complete contrast. It had been
fabricated as a replica of an English pub. The sign over the door bore
the legend 'The Victory Inn'. Licensed to sell wines, spirits and
tobacco. It had mullioned windows, and I entered through a stout
oak door. The ceilings were oak-beamed. At one end of the saloon
was a roaring fire, at the other an oak bar attended by stools upon
which the customers perched themselves. It could have been the
White Hart in Brasted, and as I downed my first pint of beer from a
pewter tankard after a long month, I felt a twinge of homesickness. I
could imagine the motives of the Gibraltar garrison who had built it
before the war. A nostalgic bit of old England in an Imperial outpost,
where servicemen could relax and recapture their past in an
ambience that reminded them of it.

Two more days passed in idle speculation about our future
destination, and then, the balloon we had been waiting for, went up.
'Allied landings in North Africa' screamed the newspaper headlines.
'British and American Commandos capture Algiers. Fighting at
Oran and Casablanca.'

As a score of British and American fighter pilots sat around the
Victory Inn bar, we raised our tankards, and drank to the best kept
secret of the war.

November 10th
With the announcement of the landings we were allowed out of
our confinement to visit the town and airstrip which was our primary
concern. Parked on one side of the latter we saw a veritable armada
of Spitfires, wing tip to wing tip, running its length. The fuselages
and wings had been crated separately, and assembled at the point of
departure, with ill-conceived tropical air/sand filters which were
completely unnecessary in North Africa, and detracted considerably
from performance which we were to discover to our substantial cost.

That evening, in the Victory Inn, we met up with a pilot from an

American squadron equipped with Spitfires who had returned from Oran to pick up a replacement.

He told us that three French Dewoitine fighters had attacked them as they were coming in to land, and shot down one of them, killing the pilot, whereupon the rest of the squadron retracted their undercarriages, gave chase and shot down the three Frenchmen. A survivor, when interrogated as to why they had attacked them, replied that the German Gestapo had threatened to kill their families in France if they didn't put up a fight. After Oran had finally capitulated, the pilot took the Americans to a hay loft where thirteen Gestapo agents were nailed to the walls.

November 11th

In the morning, we were given our marching orders, and a lorry conveyed us, together with our parachute kit bags, to the airstrip, where we got our briefing that we would be taking off in one hour's time for Algiers. We were to escort three Hudsons of Coastal Command who would lead us to our destination, fighter pilots being notoriously bad navigators. Thereafter, we were directed to a dispersal point where twelve Spitfires (tropical), fitted with long range tanks were waiting to be flown off. We stowed the only kit we had room for in our parachute bags, behind our seats, checked up on our fuel, and waited for the flag.

We watched the three Hudsons take off, then followed in close pursuit, across the Mediterranean in the direction of Algiers, with fingers crossed that we had sufficient fuel to reach it, and that our motors wouldn't quit on us.

I had left Jimmy Baraldi, one of my flight commanders, behind with the rest of the pilots to follow on later with the remaining complement of aircraft.

For the first hour, I could see land on either side of us, and a large convoy steaming eastwards. I tried not to pay any attention to my engine which my imagination tried to fool me into believing was running rough. It was always the same with me, flying over the sea, but I comforted myself with the thought that, at least, this was a, warm one. Finally, I opened my cockpit hood, telling myself that it was on account of the heat, but knowing, in truth, that it was to let in the wind whose roar would drown out my engine sound.

All of a sudden, we spotted a submarine on the surface, and the Hudsons dived down to attack it. We watched it crash-dive, as we

Jimmy Baraldi

circled above, consuming more of our limited petrol supply than, as it proved, some could afford.

After about three hours airborne, we had sighted the Algerian coast, when Mac Gilmour called on the RT that he had run out of petrol, and would have to force land. I asked him if he could make land, and he answered that he thought he could and 'cheerio for the meantime'. I knew I couldn't wait to see what happened to him, and minutes later Tommy Tinsey called to say he was in the same predicament.

As we crossed over the Bay of Algiers, losing altitude, I saw the harbour full of ships of all sorts and sizes, and heard Radio Algiers warning the harbour patrol to expect friendly aircraft from the West. Then another of the boys called to say his motor had stopped and I ordered everyone to get in and land in any way they could.

Only nine of us made the crowded airfield, and as I taxied up to a convenient-looking dispersal area, switched off and climbed out of my cockpit, I felt very tired, hungry and depressed. This was certainly not an auspicious beginning to our adventure in North Africa, and I was filled with forebodings which eventually caught up with me.

I walked towards a white square building which looked as if it should be station headquarters. The airfield was littered with aircraft of every description. Across the far side were some recently bombed-out hangars, and in front of them a number of Douglas transport planes with paratroopers sitting under their wings which sheltered them from sun or intermittent rain. Hurricanes and Spitfires seemed to be taking off and landing every minute, and I passed a three engined French aircraft and a He 111 which some ground crew had converted into their residence.

I saw Pete Hugo conferring outside the white building with Pete Powell harassed, but very glad to see our arrival. I told him I was three missing because of an interrupted journey draining our petrol. He told me food was scarce, and accommodation nil. 'Just scrounge what you can get. There are some 'K' rations around if you can track them down, and a cafe attached to the building sometimes opens.' The boys who had now caught up with me, overheard the conversation but said nothing. Just sat on the building steps, and swallowed the smoke from their cigarettes.

I asked about blankets and Pete answered negative. However, late evening, the cafe did open and we queued a half hour for some lukewarm stew that tasted how we imagined goat meat would.

Tommy Tinsey and Dick Pertwee showed up in time for the repast, but no news of Mac Gilmour, which had me worried. Tommy recounted how he had wheels-up landed and was soon surrounded by a bunch of pretty French girls. He had affected a limp to attract sympathy in which he had succeeded. Dick had fared far less romantically, having landed in the outback whence he had to walk five miles to find the nearest Allied military post where an American doctor had shaved the hair off the top of his head where the sliding hood had caught him a crack, and replaced it with a piece of sticking plaster. He looked more as if he had contracted a disease of the scalp than been *blessé à guerre*. I was beginning to feel a deep depression setting in when Pete offered me a bottle of Algerian wine and by the time I'd emptied it I felt no need for blankets and far more happily disposed towards the war.

Meanwhile, Pete, an old friend whom I'd trained with at Drem and now Wing Commander, filled me in on what the action had, so far, been. They had been bombed by about twenty Ju 88s the first day they had arrived, and shot some of them down. The French in their area were playing half-hearted allies, and some of the airfield ground crews they'd had to herd into a hangar to make up their minds whose side they wanted to be on, but the officers seemed on ours. One of the forts had fired at our ships, and after a preliminary warning a British cruiser fired a broadside at it, blowing it to pieces. Similarly, Oran had given trouble when six destroyers came sailing out of the harbour despite repeated warnings to stay put, and another of our cruisers polished them off, one after the other.

Pete then told me that the most pressing problem was at Boughie, a port town one hundred miles east, where our ships were having hell knocked out of them, and the Navy screaming for air support. Same old story as Dunkirk. Some Hurricanes were covering it from dawn, and I was to relieve them at eleven o'clock when I'd put my house in order.

Towards nightfall, Mac Gilmour turned up in an ambulance, and

I thought, Oh Christ, one down already and a flight commander to boot. He hobbled out on two sticks, but said he felt fine which he didn't look, but that his aircraft was a write-off.

While the boys fed and took care of him, I went looking for the Station Commander Edwards-Jones – EJ. as he was called by his contemporaries – to find out where we could place our casualty. When I had located him, EJ. said he could have his cot in the Control Tower and no argument. He and I would sleep on the floor. And thus was spent our first night in North Africa. Mac tossing uneasily in the CO's bed with he and I sleeping on the stone floor beside him.

I awoke at dawn from uneasy sleep and tramped across the airfield to find the boys already at our dispersal point. They had bunked down in any shelter they could find. Dispersed aircraft, and ditches loaded with human excrement, the hangars being pre-empted by our indecisive prisoners. The RAF Servicing Commandos were working on our Spitfires at which we left them to go in search of breakfast, and get our briefing for our first day's action.

Their brethren in the army were very deprecating of their nomenclature of 'Commando' until they had witnessed their feats of incredible endurance and bravery, subject to constant and unheralded machine gun and bomb attack while maintaining our aeroplanes, completely exposed, in the enemy's prime target area.

Meanwhile, I checked in at the improvised station headquarters to get my briefing from Pete Hugo, Wing Commander Flying. 111 Squadron was to mount a section patrol over Algiers in the morning, and the port of Boughie, 120 miles east of us, in the afternoon.

I led the first patrol over the port, the last one over the latter, flying along the rugged coastline, thinking, 'God help anyone who had to force-land there! As I approached Boughie, the sea was streaked with large patches of oil stretching out like the tentacles of an octopus. The bay resembled a Dante's inferno, and bombed merchant ships lay abandoned at the entrance of the harbour, flames pouring from their hulls, the water inside of which appeared to be boiling. Columns of black smoke spiralled hundreds of feet into the sky. A frigate perched defiantly on a sandbank, its ensign still flying from its masthead. But, we saw no sign of the enemy.

As dusk started to fall, I headed my section for home, only to learn on landing that the port was heavily attacked five minutes after our departure. The enemy had radar coverage where we didn't, and precipitated their attacks when they saw the coast was clear.

111 Fighter Squadron *en route* to Algeria

Mac seemed very much more lively when I went to see him in the morning. He had been provided with stretcher accommodation in a tented sick quarters and was being looked after by an American medical unit. He was very anxious to re-visit the scene of his crash landing to retrieve his kit and parachute he told me, so as the clouds were on the deck, I borrowed a vehicle and drove him.

There, I met a charming French family with a very pretty daughter who had rescued him. After a joyful reunion celebration with bottles of wine, we almost forgot what we had come for. When we got back, we found that the boys had dug themselves in, and made a dispersal hut out of empty petrol tins and a tarpaulin next door to the paratroops' transport Douglas'. One of their officers told me that they had captured Bleda and had experienced difficulty in persuading a hostile and frightened French army staff that hundreds of British aeroplanes would be pouring in at any moment. After two days of waiting for this event, three old Blenheims staggered in, one of which collapsed on landing.

The situation at Bleda was symptomatic of the French attitude to the Allied invasion in the early stages. Although most seemed glad to see us, many were afraid to collaborate, as they did not believe in the magnitude of the show, were terrified of the dreaded Gestapo and over all, backing the wrong horse, as German propaganda had convinced them we were. One time, when visiting the harbour, a French lady was standing beside me as a large convoy was pulling into the Bay. Suddenly, she grabbed and kissed me, then said, 'But, we were told that all of your ships had been sunk.'

Jimmy Baraldi and the rest of my pilots landed safely from

Gibraltar in the evening.

November 14th

I was given one hour's notice to take off for Bone with as many aircraft as I could muster, which amounted to ten. I followed the coastline and reached the town at dusk. The aerodrome looked small, and the runways uninvitingly narrow. Just as I was about to lower my wheels, I saw flak bursting over the harbour, and a Ju 88 dived out of the clouds, but dropped no bombs, so I reckoned he was on photographic reconnaissance.

I gave chase for a while, but was low on fuel, and left it to the standing patrol to catch up with him, which they did. I covered my squadron as they made their landing, then came in myself and parked on the apron in front of the control tower. Pete Hugo and Charles Appleton, the Commanding Officer, were there, awaiting my arrival. A short, stocky, huge moustached Yorkshireman joined the group. Rass Berry commanded 81 Squadron.

'Thank God you've arrived,' he greeted me. 'We've flown our arses off, most of our aircraft have been bombed or shot up, and there's no early warning system. We're sitting ducks.'

This dissertation on disaster, past and impending, was only too correct although I would have never dreamt it at the time.

Our billet proved to be a ramshackle French colonial two-storey house, not far distant. Its owners, a family of Italians, we heard, kicked out by the Commandos who had captured the airfield, must have been of pretty underprivileged stock, as the place smelt of decay from rotting floorboards and musty curtains. Our supper consisted of an unfamiliar tasting stew, dished up in porridge plates by one of the Commando's cooks who resembled a gorilla and wore a bowler that never left his head, even on a raid. When the fire needed more wood, he would break up the furniture to refuel.

I shared a room with Pete Hugo and Charles Appleton while the boys bunked in the sitting room. There were no beds, and we slept ore straw palliasses scattered around the floor. I was roused from an uneasy sleep by an invasion of lice crawling over my body, but I decided that I was too tired to care.

November 15th

Everyone was awake before dawn, and we made a weary way to our assignation with our Spitfires which I found being checked out by the Servicing Commando.

Our routine status was to be two aircraft constantly on patrol over the airfield, and two stand-by for immediate take off, with pilots in their aircraft, due to the lack of an early warning system. We scrambled when a red flare was shot into the air from the Control Tower.

Strapped in one's cockpit at readiness I likened to a nightmare when one is conscious of a predator but incapable of escape until suddenly awakened by reality which in this case was the barking of the Ack-Ack guns, signalling an enemy's approach. The tracer would reach skywards and one would press the starter button, sweating and praying for quick engine reaction. Then, push throttle hard through the gate, and a leap forward and skywards in any direction.

Our enemies continued to attack us at intervals and unheralded throughout the day with bombs, cannon and machine gun fire. The low cloud was on their side, but we succeeded in ferreting two of them out which never made home base. Between patrols, I busied myself with squadron organisation: selecting a dispersal point adjacent to land drainage ditches, setting up petrol dumps, and having a land line laid to the Control Tower so we could communicate.

I watched one of my boys try to make a landing after an attack on a Ju 88 whose rear gunner had hit him. He was holding off prior to touch down when he stalled and crashed in hideous flames. We managed to drag him out of his cockpit, only to find that he had been shot through the top of his skull. The first of our North African casualties.

Nearby ran a railway line from which we prised up the sleepers to cover the ditch we concealed ourselves in, except those on readiness and exposed in their cockpits. Sitting ducks, as Rass Berry had described it. After dusk I had accepted an invitation to have drinks with the Commandos. Their house was smaller but much cleaner than ours. Their booze was Algerian wine drawn from a two hundred litre barrel. They were an incredibly tough bunch who seemed to get a kick out of the action. I drank more than I should have, and spent the night there.

I was airborne as dawn broke to make sure that some defence was about before the bombers arrived. It was bitterly cold in my cockpit, and windscreen icing didn't help any. When the sun rose over the mountain tops, radiating its welcome warmth, I thought of a similar sensation of being in an ice-cold bath being slowly infused with hot water. I stayed up as long as my fuel would permit, but it was only after I hack landed that the first Hun appeared, and I watched my relief patrol shoot it down. I did two more patrols, but it wasn't my day.

I had made up my mind that I wouldn't spend another night in our bug-ridden billet. The Commando took pity on me, and invited me to share theirs. I knew that my boys were quite capable of fending for themselves in alternative sleeping accommodation, and some had moved into a hotel in the town, reckoning that the bombs were preferential to the bugs. That night I slept untroubled due to the panacea of Algerian wine, but regrettably awoke at first light with a gigantic hangover.

As I made my way across the airfield to our dispersal, a Ju 88 came diving out of the clouds to drop its stick of bombs directly over me, it seemed, and I ran as fast as I could in another direction. The dawn patrol was not yet airborne, and I cursed as I saw their propellers turning slowly on their uncharged starter batteries. Suddenly, there was a roar as the Merlins opened up, and two Spitfires jettisoned themselves into the air in hot pursuit.

I was on my own, on the second aerodrome patrol, when I thought that I was seeing things, and they started to attack me. I tight-turned, and they turned inside me with seemingly no effort and started taking pot shots at me. I tried every trick that Jeff Quill had taught me, but couldn't shake them off. I'd never seen aircraft like these before, and suddenly I realised that they were Italian Macchi fighters, and had heard about their manoeuvrability. I remembered when I'd first encountered the FW 190s. Then, inexplicably, when they had run rings around me, they broke off the engagement, formed line abreast, and headed for home. I followed, and, again inexplicably, they didn't bother to look behind them, allowing me to get within range and clobber them.

*

The squadron was getting acclimatised to the battle routine of standing patrols of sections, in turns, over harbour and home base, and being bombed and machine gunned, without warning, by day and by night. At night, I just prayed that a bomb hadn't got my number; by day, we could hide in our 'funk' hole, unless one was on 'readiness' patrol standby. Then we were as vulnerable as the unfortunate Servicing Commandos and the Pioneer Corps who filled in the bomb craters, totally exposed.

I saw a Spitfire of 81 Squadron swing off the runway on take-off, and decapitate four members of the Pioneers. Their faces were still animated when we picked up their heads.

Tommy Tinsey had located a monastery in the mountains where he had bought a big barrel of Algerian wine with money from his 'escape kit', the only funds we possessed. We placed this by our air-raid shelter, and attached to it a rubber tube whereby we could suck the wine, in safety, underground.

After an evening's heavy drinking with the Commandos, we decided to investigate the night life of Bone, and picked up an Arab guide to take us to a brothel. I don't think any of us intended to touch, just see, and the first two places we called on had been evacuated. But, determined to find satisfaction for his protégés, as he thought, our toothless, grinning friend said, *'Les jeunes filles Arabes, peut être?'*, and when we grinned back, named a neighbouring village in which he guaranteed us some action, but, by this time, we had had our fun, tipped him handsomely, and returned to our billets, to sleep and sober up.

Checking our maps and the order of battle the following morning, we discovered that the village he had recommended *'pour les jeunes filles Arabes'* was behind the enemy lines.

In North Africa

November 17th

I had heard a rumour that there was a French radio station somewhere near the aerodrome, and it wasn't long before I discovered it, a white square building surrounded by an olive grove about a mile from our dispersal point. When I had an hour to spare, I walked over to investigate, and upon entering the premises, found two French radio operators fiddling with transceivers and direction finders, with a huge Commando slumped in a chair, who, it transpired, was their guard. When I asked him what went on with this scene, he replied that it was a DF (direction finding) station belonging to the civil airways, and that he was installed to 'keep an eye on the Frogs to see that they didn't pass any messages that they shouldn't'. He spoke French.

When I asked him what they were now doing, he told me, just plotting the movement of enemy aircraft for their own amusement. They have observation posts still operating in the mountains. I flipped, and simultaneously a bell rang, one of the Frenchmen picked up a telephone, and started writing on a pad.

Looking over his shoulder I deciphered, 'Three Heinkel 111s approaching airfield from Cap Rosa.'

I shouted at the Commando to relay the message to the Control Tower assuming there must be a line, and was infuriated at his lethargy in reaching for another phone. 'Number's always engaged', he yawned, 'so I've given up trying.' It was engaged on this occasion. I swore, and ran all the way back to the airfield.

By nightfall we had laid down a direct land line between our headquarters and the DF station, and installed our own operators.

November 18th, 1942

I was in Station HQ conferring with Charles Appleton and Pete Hugo on the next day's action when the bell of the special phone to the DF station rang. It relayed a sighting of a formation of Ju 88s approaching the harbour, and I made a dash for my dispersal point. Within minutes the squadron was airborne, and soon after we saw the flak start to burst in a torrent over the harbour.

We had to keep well clear until the bombs had gone down, and the bombers turned for home base, then we went in pursuit, and thanks to our cannons wrought havoc on the attackers, who had escaped the anti-aircraft fire.

*

Thereafter, the enemy became more cautious, timing their

assaults before dawn and after dusk in their knowledge that we had no night fighters in the area, and multiple daylight bomber raids came to an end over Bone.

Night was a different story.

I remember, one time, yakking with some of the boys about fatalism; how it didn't matter where one was if a bomb had one's number on it, it was going to hit you, sure as heaven and hell, and there was nothing one could do about it. And yet, one would feel a sense of complete security when once the dividing perimeter road of the airfield was crossed, and one had reached some roof over one's head, even if only half a mile distant from the target area.

We had all the instincts of the ostrich. As long as we could hide our heads from a hostile sky, beneath a cover, however fragile, we felt perfectly secure.

November 21st

Our daily briefing included what was going on with the Eighth Army as well as ours, and we knew that 'Monty' was racing towards Tunis. Our army had pushed forward into the Tebourba area, and had reached the outskirts. To try and stem this tide of advance, the Germans were using more and more aircraft, mostly fighters, to attack British transport on the roads leading to the front line, with serious effect, and the cries came back, as they had at Dunkirk, 'Where is the RAF?'

For our answer, we only had two squadrons to cover the whole of the First Army, of which 75% of the planes were unserviceable. Our ground crews and spares had not yet arrived, and our major commitment was the protection of the harbours and the aerodrome. We had little time left over for army support up front. However, I decided to compromise, and started to come up against groups of fighters, the latest Me 109s and the deadly FW 190s. Against these formidable aircraft, we had only our out-dated tropical Spitfires Mark Vs with which to challenge them.

Our enemy had the advantage of speed, but more important, height, the paramount element of air fighting. In order to combat this, I developed a new fighter tactic of an undulating flight path taken independently by sections which varied by a thousand feet altitudes. This had the effect of confusing the enemy as to where the core of the squadron lay as it was never on the same level, which resulted in many surprise and successful attacks.

November 22nd

I had caught a touch of the indigenous fever which was rampant, and was trying to snatch an hour's sleep by dispersal, when the alarm siren went off, and I ran for my aircraft. As I was fastening my parachute and harness, my mechanic yelled, 'You'll never make it, Sir', and started to run, pointing wildly towards the sky.

Looking upwards, I saw about a dozen fighter bombers diving down towards the aerodrome, released myself from the captivity of my cockpit, and made for the nearest cover. This happened to be a truck, parked at the side of the airfield which some Arabs were filling with stones. As I dived under it, they followed and plunged on top of me, a gibbering, odoriferous mass of humanity. Simultaneously, I heard the roar of aero engines, and the clatter of machine gun fire before the first bomb struck and exploded. The detonation stung my body like a whiplash, and momentarily blinded me.

Then, looking up, I saw a Spitfire tearing down the runway towards me. The pilot had just retracted his undercarriage when a second projectile hit directly in front of him. The aircraft staggered, hit the ground and skated along the runway surface, straight towards me, with flames pouring from its punctured petrol tanks. When it had come to rest, I watched with horror the pilot struggle but fail to extricate himself from this inferno, and I was too paralysed either by shock or fear to go to his assistance. I will never know the truth, and a guilty conscience that it was fear, has haunted me ever since.

When the last bomb had fallen, and the noise of aero engines and machine gun fire subsided, I walked over to what remained of my Spitfire; the first bomb had hit it, and I saw it was a write-off. The burned-out aircraft of my comrade I avoided, but glimpsed a charred scarecrow arm, which seemed to beckon me, reproachfully. An inspection of the truck which had sheltered me, showed scars from cannon, shrapnel and machine gun bullets, but I had emerged unscathed. I marvelled at my escape.

Jimmy Baraldi, Mac Gilmour and Bill Draper turned up in the evening with the rearguard of the squadron in a motorised convoy which also carried our much needed spare parts for our aircraft. It had taken them three days by the coastal road from Algiers, and their description of the scenery made me long for a few days' leave, and an open sports car more than anything on earth. Jimmy had got hold of a 15 cwt truck which had been lent him by the army, so he told me with a grin, and I didn't probe deeper into his acquisition, as my feet were blistered from walking.

I told my two flight commanders that from now on they could share my load, and determined to take it more easy.

Mac Gilmour and Bill Draper

November 23rd-24th

I had been running a temperature and decided to move to a hotel, and said any who wanted could join me, but most opted for the wide open spaces, except Jimmy who deplored discomfort. That night, I climbed between sheets for the first time since landing in Africa, and despite the multitude of blankets I was shivering with cold, and I realised that the local fever had caught up with me.

The crisis came, I broke into a sweat which swamped my bed, and thereafter, I slept for twelve hours, in the knowledge that my flight commanders could take care of the action.

When I woke, I took a cold shower, dressed leisurely, breakfasted and strolled down to the harbour, where several merchant ships were docked, and unloading war cargo. A couple of destroyers lay at anchor in the bay. I then thumbed a lift up to the airfield and arrived just in time to see Tinsey crash-land. He had mixed with some 109s, got one, and another got him, so the score was one all, and everybody happy.

That evening, we were carousing in the town with some
Commando officers when a fight broke out in a neighbouring
tavern, between some Argyll and Sutherlands and American GIs
besotted with Algerian wine, of which someone had hastened to
advise us. Straightaway, the Commando Major rose to his feet,
loosened his ·45, and went to investigate, I following to witness
whether their action lived up to its reputation.

On entering the tavern the scene looked explosive. Men
crouched behind tables and chairs, some with knives, ready to spring
at one another's throats, it would seem. The Commando took it in at
first glance, took his gun by the barrel and struck the largest
belligerent he could see unconscious. As he sprang towards another
of the opposing side, the soldier held up his hands in capitulation,
dropping his knife. The confrontation was over, as suddenly as it had
begun, the Major holstered his gun, and told the antagonists to shake
hands, or get out, before he called up his boys. When peace was
restored, he revived his victim, and bought him a drink.

A story I heard, at this time from a Commando sergeant, maybe
apocryphal, who claimed to have been on a raid on a French brothel
in the Pas de Calais, which the underground leaked was patronised
by Gestapo officers. With blackened faces, half a dozen of his unit
had been launched in rubber dinghies from a submarine to
assassinate them, and on entering the premises separated the men
from the girls on either side of the main room, whereupon their CO
had drawled, 'Gentlemen, this is going to slay you', then knocked
them off with his tommy gun.

There was almost unlimited scope for enterprising scroungers,
Tommy Tinsey and Canadian Bill Draper formed what they called
'The Combine', which guaranteed to procure anything from a bunch
of bananas, to a motor vehicle. I was presented with a very fine
model in Peugeots – a smart little four door saloon which had been
liberated from some Italians. Other 'Combine' acquisitions were
three motor cycles, and an assortment of automatic weapons with
which the boys formed quite a commendable anti-aircraft consortium.

Someone had got hold of a Tricolour flag which we flew from
the front of our truck, much to the delight of the French inhabitants
of Bône.

November 25th

We were told that the army were going to make an all out attempt to capture Tunis and Bizerta, and they asked for air support from dawn until dusk. We mounted standing patrols all day without contact with the enemy, and watched the trucks and lorries tearing along the road to Mejez el Bab, and further east, occasional puffs of mortar fire.

In late afternoon, I spotted a formation of Ju 87s, called Mac to act as top cover and led my section to attack them. The 87s dived for the ground when they saw us coming, and started a frantic evasive action, twisting like corkscrews. I picked on one of them who practically turned himself inside out with contortions before I blew his wing off.

I finished off another before I ran out of ammo and became a spectator, at which time I realised we were plumb over the Tunis airfield where the boys were now shooting it out in the circuit. The ack-ack didn't dare fire for fear of hitting their own side.

Just after we'd joined up and were heading for home, I spotted a formation of 88s approaching from the sea, and calling the boys to follow me, headed straight at them, although we had run out of ammo. Not knowing this, and in panic, they unloaded their bombs which landed harmlessly in no man's land, and then took off in every direction. They must have been fielding their third division.

November 27th

The CO had decided that the Hotel de Nice, into which most of the boys had now moved, was too near the harbour for safety, and had requisitioned another hotel further out along the bay. The place was unfurnished, 'The Combine' soon rectified that by raids on blitzed and evacuated houses. However, most of the boys were unwilling to move out from their establishment, and several had set up house with accommodating French ladies in the town. I tried to set an example, but the CO agreed with me that there was no point in forcing the issue, as taking everything into consideration, one place was just as likely to get hit as another.

After dark, the 88s plastered the harbour, and when I arrived to collect the boys at dawn, everyone had his bags packed, and was ready for the move.

November 28th

Patrolled the road between Sejennane and Mateur, and watched our infantry moving along the dusty highway. Saw about forty

111 Squadron pilots

Fortresses thousands of feet above us, making their way towards Bizerta. They sailed on like a mighty armada, making their smoke trails in the sky.

We were running out of fuel when three FW 190s attacked us from above and then pulled up again as we turned into them. The only thing we could do. They knew that our tropical Spits were no match for them, as long as they didn't mix it in a turn. When they repeated the performance, I told the boys to hit the deck and make their own way home.

I stayed for their second attack in a wide turn, and as they overshot and started climbing, I hauled back on my stick, until almost hanging on my propeller, got their arse end Charlie in my sights and blasted him, then fled after my squadron of Spitfires being put to flight by three of the enemy. What would the army think?

When I landed back at the airfield, the ground crews told me they had been attacked by five Ju 88s which had blown up two Hurribombers, which had landed from a raid to refuel. I felt exhausted and decided to make an early night of it, leaving Mac Gilmour and Jimmy Baraldi to attend the G/C's evening briefing. I reached the hotel as the sirens started up, and stood in the garden watching the dark shapes of the enemy bombers as they swooped down on the ships in the harbour like giant birds of prey.

The explosions of the bombs were almost drowned by the roar of the anti-aircraft barrage. Tracers flickered in the sky like a monstrous fireworks display. I felt I was witnessing some devil's carnival. Instinctively, I put my fingers in my ears. Then, an orderly rushed up to me, and shouted that I was wanted on the telephone. That the airfield had been blitzed and the Group Captain hit, amongst others, and that more ambulances were needed.

Pete Hugo, on the other end of the phone confirmed the disaster, and I said I'd come right on up with another ambulance and the squadron doc. When we reached the field I first saw that our HQ had been hit, then Charles Appleton lying on the apron outside surrounded by some of the boys. He was screaming with pain and one leg was hanging by a thread.

We scooped him up and put him in our ambulance, and as we drove off, I saw a flak truck had also been hit, and bits of bodies scattered all over and around it. I drove up to the field hospital, a couple of miles away, as the driver had been sick, and seemed incapable. Then I left him with the Doc and got a ride back.

Pete told me that when the attack started, they were in the middle of their briefing, and Charles had run out onto the apron to direct the defence when the bomb near-missed him.

'We'll hold no more bloody conferences on the airfield,' he added grimly.

November 29th

The standing patrols brought down a couple of Ju 88s who'd attacked the harbour in the morning, and I jumped a 109 when on a squadron sweep over Mateur in the afternoon. I don't know what he was doing on his own, and I thought, at first he was a decoy, so told the boys stay up top and cover me while I took him. He could never have known what hit him. He disintegrated in a sheet of orange flame.

In the evening, I went up to the field hospital to see Charles. Tinsey who was still u/s with shrapnel wounds drove me in the Peugeot. It had started to pour with torrential rain. The camp was pitched about a hundred yards off the road on sloping ground. Rows of drab-looking marquees, shoulder to shoulder, accommodated the dying and wounded. Hastily laid stone paths enabled medical orderlies and doctors to pass from operating theatres to sick bays without sinking up to their ankles in mud.

Stacks of medical supplies stamped with the Red Cross lay strewn around in the open. Broken open packing cases revealed enamel utensils, broken medicine bottles and bandages soiled with mud. Two white-masked surgeons came out of a marquee as I passed, and I could see their hands shaking as they peeled off their rubber gloves. They looked as if they could hardly keep their eyes open.

A body was carried out of the theatre, the head swathed in dripping bandages, and the torso wrapped in a coarse army blanket. I asked one of them where I could find the G/C and was directed to a tent up the line. As I approached, I saw his batman coming out, and when he recognised me, he whispered, 'Thank God you've come, Sir. He desperately needs someone to cheer him up.'

The inside of the tent was almost devoid of light. The air smelt of a mixture of sweat, blood, disinfectant and dysentery. Charles lay, wrapped in army blankets, on a camp bed. His face was a greenish yellow, and his cheeks were drawn with pain. I thought, at first, that he was sleeping, but he opened his eyes when I bent over him, and whispered my name. I asked him how he felt, although it was obvious, and added some inadequate platitudes of condolence, to which he replied and continued to repeat:

'I've made such a bloody fool of myself. I'll never be of any use again. It's my leg, you know. I've lost my leg. All my bloody fault. Should have listened to your advice. Never should have held briefing on the airfield. My fault.'

He rambled on, doped with morphia, eyes closed and throwing his head from one side to the other as each spasm of pain gripped him, sucking in each breath and expelling it in a gasp.

When I thought he had passed out, he suddenly said, 'How are the boys bearing up?' and when I answered fine, he added, 'Good bunch. I let 'em down. Tell Pete to take over. Sound chap, Pete. One of the best. Good friend of yours, I know. I shall never fly again. Going to miss it like blazes.'

I told him that was nonsense. To think of Douglas Bader, and he then said I was right and repeated Douglas Bader several times before an orderly came in and beckoned me to leave. As I raised the tent flap to let myself out, he groaned,

'Thank you for coming to see me, Tony. I'm feeling a lot better now. Tell the boys I'll be back soon.' But, as I left him, I knew that he wouldn't.

I met the surgeon on the path and asked how the wound was healing. He told me there was a danger of gangrene, but to hope for the best. I passed a verminous-looking bunch of Arabs putting stones on the path, and thought about gangrene.

On the way back to camp, we blew a tyre, and after a series of sickening swerves we came to a stop with one wheel over the railway line. We had nearly got the wheel changed when a train suddenly appeared around the bend, moving slowly but inexorably towards us. The driver pulled the whistle and waved frantically at us from the cab window, while we waved back to try and indicate our dire predicament. Then followed a hissing of applied brakes but resulting in little loss of inertia before the engine struck and ripped away a side of the Peugeot, carrying it on its journey. We thumbed our way back to the airfield, leaving our chariot forever behind us.

To add to our misfortunes and depression, that evening the Army liaison officer called on us at our hotel to say that the troops had been heavily ground strafed and seen no British fighters when they were needed, and I realised that the Hun had assessed our petrol limitations, and launched his assaults accordingly. We would have to figure out a way to counteract this, and I knew this could only mean a move up closer to their front line. That night I got very drunk.

November 30th

In the afternoon we shared our patrol line with a squadron of USAAF Lightnings. They were flying Hendon Air Display formation, and had obviously never seen any enemy in their lives. If I'd had their wavelength, I would have warned them to go home before someone spotted them as sitting ducks.

Suddenly, I saw two 109s circle them like vultures, selecting their prey, taking their time. They were thinking just as I was, I reckoned, and forgot about anything else. As they started their attack on their unsuspecting enemy, I started ours and the 109s never looked behind, into the sun, until it was too late. As we turned for home base, running out of fuel, we saw the Lightnings sail on in close formation completely unaware of what had been going on around them. I made a note to get in touch with their Group Commander as soon as I'd landed, and tell him the facts of life, or death, but it was comforting to see some American support, at last.

We had been expecting some replacement aircraft for several days, but it was with no small concern that we witnessed their arrival, seven of them, after returning to the airfield as the sun was setting. It was hard enough for us who knew the hazards of the area, to land in semi-darkness, and as I watched them in the circuit I had my doubts of their total success.

Then, I heard the sirens start to scream, and the Ack-Ack start to bark, whereupon we jumped into our truck, beat it down the road a fair distance before pulling up under some trees to watch the inevitable catastrophe.

A Ju 88 came hurtling across the field letting go a stick of bombs, scattering the circling Spitfires who were trying to put down, then attacked one with its wheels down which crashed in flames. Thereafter pandemonium as more Junkers appeared, more flak was thrown, more bombs were dropped and the airfield lit up by incendiaries which some pilots mistook for a flare path. There was nothing we could do about it, so when a lull came in the action, we headed for the town flat out.

Home and dry in our hotel, we learned that the replacements were not for us, but for an American squadron that was moving in, and that all seven aircraft and several pilots written off. The American squadron commander, Colonel Allison, swore he'd fix the Ops bastards who'd scheduled their arrival from Algiers at the hour they had, and I couldn't have agreed with him more.

December 1st

A dismal beginning to the Christmas month. The airfield looked like a second-hand junk yard when we saw it at dawn. Crashed and burned out aircraft everywhere, including a Wellington bomber which had crash-landed in an adjoining field, after an unsuccessful attempt to locate the runways. The flak truck which had been guarding our dispersal area was a twisted mass of metal, and the gunners strewn around in fragments. Our runways were pitted with delayed action bombs, and our first priority was to remove our aircraft before they exploded. I told two of our replacement pilots to taxi them out of the danger area. They had to learn sometime.

A squadron of Bisleys came in to refuel on their way to bomb the road just west of Mateur. I met their CO, Malcome, and chatted to some of his crew. They chain-smoked incessantly, and their nervousness I found contagious. I asked Malcome how they'd been doing, and he replied OK except that he'd been through a complete squadron of pilots already. When I questioned him on escort fighters, he replied, rather bitterly, that they were never given any, that they were supposed to rely on cloud cover, and more often than not, there wasn't any.

This time we escorted him on his raid, shot down two 109s, and brought all the bombers back in one piece. I enjoyed that trip more than any I had done, so far. I felt like a boy scout that had done his good turn for the day.

I had been asked to dinner by the commanding officer of a Commando battalion in a neighbouring hotel they had made their officers' mess. I discovered it to be a small party including Randolph Churchill. The food consisted of compo rations supplemented with fresh eggs and vegetables. The Colonel seemed to me typical of the old school and reminisced about pig-sticking and polo in Poonah. My fellow guests completely ignored me while they argued about Lord Beaverbrook, one attacking Janet's father quite vitriolically in respect to his private and political affairs, with Randolph defending him, though I thought somewhat half-heartedly, whilst getting steadily drunker on Algerian wine as dinner progressed, neither knowing that I knew the tycoon and loved his daughter.

I tried to eavesdrop on their conversation and at the same time respond hospitably to my host's stories which gave me indigestion.

My fellow guest continued to hold forth about the Beaver's adulterous affairs and financial dealings, explaining while brandishing his eating utensils where his capital was secreted including endowment funds for his mistresses. When I got back to our billet, one of the 81 Squadron pilots who had been missing for several days had just shown up, and regaled me with the story of his capture and ultimate escape.

He had been shot down behind the German lines at Mateur and taken prisoner by a patrol of a dozen infantry, short of food and ammunition and retreating as fast as they could. The young pilot, having determined his plan of escape, pretended to develop a violent case of malaria, shivering and shaking so realistically that he convinced the Germans he was at death's door.

There were hundreds of British and American Commandos and Paras closing in, he told them, and that if they didn't take care of him, when inevitably captured he would denounce them for cruelty to their prisoner of war, and have them all shot, which the guileless infantrymen had believed. They were aware of the reputation of these shock troops, gave the prisoner their blankets for a bed, and when he insisted, carried him on their backs.

On the second day of this treatment, the pilot awoke to find he had been deserted, and walked back to Allied lines.

Dick Pertwee and Bill Davis of 111 Squadron

December 3rd

Did our standard patrol over the front line, and the Hun was out to catch us, with a prepared booby trap.

Two 109s came down through a hole in the cloud base, fast circled our six pack, and zoomed on up again. A sprat to catch a mackerel, I thought, as I followed them, telling the boys to stay down. It proved as I had suspected. On emerging above cloud, I spotted about twenty 'snappers' circling a thousand feet overhead, so beat a hasty retreat to join my own side.

In the afternoon we were given our instructions to move up to Souk el Arba the next day where a landing strip had been prepared. The road party was to travel by night to avoid strafing.

Two ambulances from the field hospital showed up and parked on the apron in front of our HQ, in anticipation of the arrival of ambulance planes from Algiers. They were filled with wounded, some of whom had been hit on the airfield, including Charles Appleton. The planes hadn't arrived, and I had time to say goodbye to him, and try to cheer him up.

Though drugged, he appeared to be suffering considerable pain, and kept on asking why they were being kept waiting, why the planes hadn't arrived. Then he cried he couldn't stand any more pain, any more bombs near him, and that they'd never reach Algiers before dark.

When the Ack-Ack started up, I told him I'd have the

ambulances moved out of the target area, and the driver to take his ambulance a couple of miles up the road and bring it back again, hoping that this subterfuge would have the effect I hoped it would. Then, I bade him goodbye, and good luck, left him and walked across the field to my dispersal area, praying that the enemy would not attack the ambulance planes.

December 4th-5th

Souk el Arba. A low, barren, oval plateau surrounded on all sides by mountain ranges, and bisected by a winding river. A single track railway connected the little towns of Guardemaou, Souk el Arba and Souk el Khemis. The airfield was nothing more than a cultivated field bounded by the main road to Tunis on its northern boundary, and cart tracks to the south. The ground bore witness of a recent attack – bomb craters, and burned-out aircraft.

Rough and ready slit trenches around the perimeter reminded me that Souk was only twenty miles behind the front line. Having dispersed my Spitfire, I walked over to a white square house which I suspected was the improvised station HQ, and I was right.

There I met some pilots of an Army CoOp squadron, the only occupying force, until our arrival. They flew tiny little monoplanes which looked like butterflies from the air. I was invited to spend the night with them which I accepted, and was conveyed in a truck to the perimeter of the field where they had pitched two tents adjacent to a large and deep slit trench.

Our evening meal consisted of tinned sausage meat and fresh eggs purchased from the itinerant Arabs, and cooked over a stove improvised from a petrol tin filled with stones and earth and drenched with a hundred octane fuel. We fed in the open, sitting on sand bags around a packing case which served as our table.

The sun had disappeared behind the mountains by the time we had finished, and stars were beginning to appear in the African sky. It was becoming intensely cold as we made our final preparations for the night. I was invited to share a tent with three of the boys who had gone to a lot of trouble to rig up a stretcher on which they piled six army blankets. They warned me that I'd need them all, and if attacked in the night, to take them with me to the slit trench as they couldn't get any filthier.

Smoking our final cigarettes before turning in, I asked their CO how they'd been doing, and he didn't answer for quite a while. His face was drawn, ears alert, as if listening for something to break the intense silence of this wilderness. Then he said he thought he'd heard an aeroplane, but it must have been imagination. They'd had a pretty rough time, he continued, from constant attack from fighter bombers, and that he'd lost a lot of his pilots, but he didn't know whether to flak or fighters; two had gone missing that day.

I slept fitfully through the night. It was bitterly cold, despite my blankets, and a damp mist crept in through the tent flap. My brain turned over my plans for the morrow. Dispersal point, a telephone line to our improvised HQ, food, and petrol supplies. The Hun's tactics were still a worry. His diving and climbing manoeuvres with his aircraft performance far superior to that of our tropical Spitfires.

It was with relief that I greeted the first light of dawn, and without waiting for breakfast, tramped across the airfield to our dispersal point. There, I found my boys feverishly erecting tents between two Arab settlements. Hygienically, the place they had selected couldn't have been worse. Filthy, half-clad Arabs wandered around the encampment watching our activities with great interest. On the other hand, here was natural camouflage, and there were deep irrigation trenches surrounding us on all sides. It was sufficient distance from our dispersed aircraft, the prime enemy target, to be reasonably safe from ground strafing, and, with careful planning, could be made to blend perfectly with the environment.

The road party turned up in the middle of the morning with transport and equipment. By midday we had collected blankets and food supplies from our trucks, erected our tents, built a field kitchen and made sanitary arrangements. Then, I got a field telephone laid from the HQ block to my tent.

In the afternoon, we made our first sortie from Souk el Arba, to cover an Army CoOp plane making a reconnaissance of enemy machine-gun emplacements in the Sejennane hills. I watched it flitting in and out of the valleys west of Mateur, and didn't envy the intrepid aviator his dangerous task. It wasn't until we had escorted him safely home that we were attacked from above by a flight of 109s.

Making use of their initial height they followed their standard tactics of a lightning pass, then a pull-up whence they'd come. I turned the squadron into a defensive circle with pairs of aircraft spread out in depth, the tactic I had developed, and with grim delight watched two 109s dive to attack the tail end Charlies who were now a thousand feet below me.

They missed them in their turn, and, pulling up, I was waiting for them, slipped in behind the second Hun and blasted him. When the other 109s came down for their revenge they didn't know where to locate our unit, and found themselves being attacked from every direction at our optimum altitude and with our superior manoeuvrability. Two more went down in a dog fight, then, getting short on fuel I told the boys to hit the deck and make for home.

Soon after, I heard a cry on the RT from someone who'd been badly hit and was being left behind. I told the boys to keep going, and swung back on my tracks to encounter a pursuing 109 closing on our lame duck, and met him head on, finishing my remaining ammunition. I had no idea whether I had hit him, but he certainly disappeared. When we finally got back to the airfield, I found a pretty shaken bunch of fighter pilots. Bill Williams, for whom I'd turned back, had been wounded by a cannon shell, and Jimmy Waring was missing.

At least, I had confirmed my theory that the squadron must fly in depth, to counteract the superiority of the 109 and FW 190s and when attacked or attacking, the leader of each pair would act independently and at his own discretion. Somewhat self-satisfied with my marksmanship, I had my armourers remove my two outboard machine guns to reduce aircraft weight.

At two o'clock in the morning, Jimmy Waring rolled up in a Jeep in the custody of an American GI. He had force-landed unhurt, with a bullet in the glycol tank.

December 5th

We were kept pretty busy over the battle area all day, but few contacts were made. The Hun was sticking to his policy of attacking only when he saw us turn for home, short of fuel. His radar read us like a book, whilst we had none. We badly needed the assistance of a second squadron. The rear guard of our personnel drove up in convoy at midday, our truck having safely transported our barrel of wine and several cases of whisky from Bône.

A Boston bomber, returning from an aborted raid on the airfield at Bizerta, force-landed by our dispersal point. The bomb-aimer had been hit in the head by flak, and died as we lifted him out of his turret. A few minutes later, a Hurribomber spun in, for reasons unknown, and started burning, within a short distance of the Boston which was still bombed up.

111 Squadron and the press

I mustered all available hands to propel the bomber away from the conflagration. It was accomplished at the double. Then we went to work on the barrel of wine, and moved it adjacent to the 'command' slit trench, as the sun was setting. The dead bomb-aimer had been put in the ambulance which I retained to accommodate the crew for the night too.

Next, I opened up two bottles of whisky and we settled down to some steady drinking while our Mess cook got acquainted with our improvised petrol tin stove, and broke out some compo rations. When we had all eaten and drunk our fill, with sleep beckoning, we escorted our now maudlin and somewhat lachrymose uninvited guests to bunk down beside their dead comrade.

December 6th

On our second patrol, we ran right into a squadron of 109s and got stuck into them. The boys carried out our new tactics to the letter, and we soon had the Huns exactly where we wanted them. A free-for-all dog-fight ensued for about twenty minutes, during which time we destroyed four and damaged two more. Tushington had to force land with a bullet which punctured his glycol tank.

After supper, we celebrated our victory with red Algerian wine and community singing, under the African stars.

December 7th

Once again, we got our marching orders to move further up towards the front line. I took Jimmy with me as interpreter, and set off for Souk el Khemis to choose our new camp-sight and dispersal area. The landing ground proved to be another large cultivated field similar to Souk el Arba, but upon which the Pioneer Corps were hastily laying a wire mesh runway over the slush surface. There was no vestige of cover whatsoever, and our new Group Captain Ronnie Lees had given me orders that our living site must be at least two miles from the airfield.

We made various enquiries at neighbouring farm houses, and, at length, decided upon a small one surrounded by a spinney which would afford sufficient camouflage for our tents. Having chosen a dispersal point by the one solitary tree on the field, I sent an advance party forward with petrol supplies, picks and shovels, with instructions to dig themselves in before the Spitfires arrived to attract the enemy's attention to our new abode.

As I was directing operations a squadron of FW fighter bombers flew over us on their way to Souk el Arba. It was only about ten miles down the road, and when the bombs fell, we could see the dust rise into the air. On their way back, I prayed that they would not spot us, when they flew over, as we had nowhere to hide our heads, let alone bodies.

When the last had disappeared, I summoned the working party which had wisely dispersed itself as far from their vehicles as possible and told them this was a lesson they'd better learn. To make their own cover by digging like hell, then emulate moles, and live underground whenever possible.

When Jimmy and I got back to Souk el Arba, we discovered that our ground defences, in their aiming to shoot down the FWs, had enfiladed our dispersal point, and shot up three aeroplanes.

That night the rain came down in torrents, and battered against the sides of our tents, making sleep difficult. My straw palliasse bed and army blankets, made up on the ground, absorbed the water like a sponge and turned the earth to mud.

December 8th

Arriving at dispersal at dawn, we discovered that our aircraft had disappeared up to their axles in a quagmire and it was impossible to move them. I took this opportunity of revisiting our new camp with Jimmy Baraldi, to set in motion our movement operation.

We called in at the local French HQ which was billeted in a large farm not far distant and who didn't seem too pleased to see us. However, after some lukewarm handshaking we enquired about a potential billet for ourselves, and were given their directions to another farmstead which we found was just over the two mile distance requirement from the airstrip which the G/C had ordered.

However, upon arrival, we discovered that the farmyard had been wired off as a POW camp, and the German prisoners looked even less pleased to see us, and only dilatorily guarded by the Poilus. The farm owner, a Monsieur Colomba, proved a genial host and advised us of a neighbouring small-holding of his which had been occupied by a tenant who had recently departed, and volunteered to show it to us. He produced a smart little convertible from his garage, and we followed him to another farmstead, a little further out, but far more suitable for our requirements. It consisted of two cottages and several barns surrounded by trees, with an adjoining spinney which could provide ample cover for our tents and vehicles.

After further enquiries of our host, we learned that the previous occupant had been an electrical engineer who had lived there alone for several years, been taken ill with appendicitis just before the Allied landings, gone to Tunis for an operation, and hadn't been heard of since. He was an Italian, and Monsieur suspected a spy, so we had no compunction about moving in.

The other cottage was also occupied by an Italian, also suspect, according to our host, and when introduced we noticed that his wife was heavy with child. He looked a pretty sinister case, so taking advantage of this situation, Jimmy volunteered the services of our squadron doctor and ambulance at the appropriate time, patting the holster of his ·38 suggestively to indicate that we would stand no hanky-panky.

The cottage consisted of only two bedrooms and a parlour-cum-kitchenette, but to us it seemed utopia. Fully furnished, scrupulously clean, but above all including electric light and a magnificent wireless set. I soon had a guard on the place, armed with a tommy-gun, and orders to shoot anyone who dared dispute our claim, and who looked even more sinister than our neighbour.

In the afternoon we went on an expedition into the mountains to find a monastery Monsieur Colomba had told us produced some of the finest wines in the country, and after a ten-mile drive up bumpy mountain roads, we arrived at our destination which appeared more like a vast distillery operated by monks. Our requirements were expeditiously attended to by an old 'lag' from Aberdeen who was a fugitive from justice for many years. We filled up the truck with brandy and every assortment of wine for which we paid a pittance from the money in our escape kits.

On our way back, we passed convoys of tanks and motorised infantry moving up to the front line, all in excellent spirits despite the rain, and we wished them good luck.

December 9th

The rain continued to pour in torrents, and it was impossible to move our aircraft, so we continued to transfer our ground staff, leaving a skeleton flight at el Arba.

I decided that the maximum sleeping accommodation that the cottage could cope with was four pilots per bedroom, while the rest of the boys would have to sleep in tents or on floors. Mac Gilmour, Jimmy, Dick Pertwee and myself took the best room, Mac and Jimmy sharing the large double bed, while Dick and I had camp ones. The rest slept on palliasses strewn about the flagstoned parlour.

December 10th

The rain continued to pour, and our aircraft sank deeper into the mud. However, our new camp was beginning to take shape, and we all kept busy with allotted tasks. The pilot boys soon realised that there was more for them to do than fly their Spitfires and drink their wine.

The Intelligence Officer appointed himself Mess Secretary and having found an excellent cook from amongst the men, improvised an inaugural evening meal composed basically of compo rations supplemented with new laid eggs and fresh vegetables to celebrate our house warming.

Monsieur Colomba was our first invited guest.

December 11th

The aircraft were still bogged down, so I decided to take the day off when I had finished my rounds of the camp and inspected the dispersal point. I wandered down to the Colombas' farm. Everything seemed so quiet and peaceful after the last few hectic days. The whole valley bathed in an aura of tranquillity, and the occasional glimpses of sunshine reflected off the whitewashed farm buildings lent a momentary sense of security. The farmstead was modern and clean, and I envied the animals which it harboured their life of peace and domesticity.

In the afternoon, I took Jimmy and a couple of the boys on an expedition to find another vineyard on the road to Beja. We drove like hell, keeping a sharp look-out for enemy aircraft. The road was showing signs of wear from the continual stream of military traffic, and large pot holes pitted the surface. When we reached the vineyard, we found the unhappy remnants of an armoured car company preparing to bivouac. They turned out to be Americans who had been badly shot up the day before, and forced to retreat during the night. Most of their cars had got stuck in the mud and abandoned. They had lost their unit, and doubted whether they would see any of them again. They complained bitterly that they never saw a British or American plane, and that they had been continuously ground-strafed. When they did meet a pilot he was in search of liquor. We tried to explain that the same mud which bogged down his armoured cars had an even more debilitating effect on our aircraft.

It was a depressing encounter, and we returned to our airfield with heavy hearts and a huge barrel of wine.

December 12th

After a struggle in which all hands took part, we managed to drag the last Spitfire out of the mud. In the afternoon we were called upon to escort some Hurribombers to Mateur, but previously I had carried out some taxying trials on the wire mesh runways, and found it necessary to carry an airman on the tail to prevent the aircraft tipping onto its nose, until the moment of take-off, when we waved him off. When the squadron had just got airborne in a left-hand circuit, I looked back to see to my horror that Tommy Tinsey still had his man pinned to his *empennage* and his aircraft bucking like a wild west bronco. He must have forgotten to wave him away. When I warned him of the predicament on the RT, he answered that he was well aware of it, and couldn't 'shake the bugger off'.

I told him to make a landing with plenty of speed to prevent stalling, which he managed precariously to accomplish. The airman was tossed off on making contact with the ground, and got away with only a broken leg.

That evening I drank a quarter of a bottle of whisky before I tore Tinsey off a monumental strip for carelessness, and threatened to kick him out of the squadron. This had been only one of a succession of his 'blacks' and ill-discipline, but he promised to reform so I forgave him.

The airman became quite a hero to his mates, and was delighted to be invalided out of the front line.

December 14th

No 152 Squadron had moved up to Souk el Arba to make up a

wing, commanded by a crazily brave New Zealander, 'Sheep' Gilroy. Peter Hugo had been moved back to Ops in Algiers, and we hoped we'd get some more realistic mission briefing from Command HQ from now on in, as he knew and could sympathise with our desperate situation in the front lines.

Sheep led the Wing over Tunis and Bizerta fast which resulted in everyone getting split up. The flak was murder, and I was forced to break back to avoid the worst of it. A couple of Huns jumped 152, and I heard some panic calls on the RT but we had lost them. Mixed it with some others, but without any kills I could confirm. There seemed to be an unusual amount of shipping in the lake, which probably accounted for the amount of lead which had been hurled at us.

In the evening, I made the usual pilgrimage to el Arba for the next day's briefing with Mac and Jimmy. We'd acquired a Humber shooting break, and we took it in turns to sit on the roof spotting for ground strafing 109s and FWs. I was beginning to loathe the sight of Souk el Arba, and life had begun to develop into a game of musical chairs, everyone moving about from place to place, keeping a continual eye on the nearest slit trench, and as soon as the Ack-Ack started up, we made a dash for it. I began to find myself sidling along walls and scrambling in ditches as we moved about.

December 15th

Escorted squadrons of Liberators and Fortresses to bomb the docks at Tunis and Bizerta. The bombers flew at maximum altitude, and we could hardly get our old Spits up to cover them. The flak was pretty hot, but the bombers drew most of it. Very few enemy fighters came up, and those we dealt with.

In the evening, some Press Correspondents came to visit us at Khemis. We pushed out a boat for them, and had to put Bill Mundy and Wilkerson to bed in the ambulance. The Adjutant broke the news that all our kit had been torpedoed which meant that we'd lost everything except what we had stowed in our parachute bags and carried in our Spitfires from Gibraltar.

I was particularly sorry to have lost a favourite shot-gun given me by my mother, with which she had shot a leopard in India off the back of an elephant, she had told me. I had never figured who was on whose back.

December 16th

Escorted Hurribombers to attack a gun battery that had been
knocking hell out of a Guards' position at Medjez el Bab. The boys
were pretty accurate with their bombs, and while the Hun gunners
were recovering from initial shock, I took the squadron down, and
we machine-gunned anything still moving. In the evening, we had
another party with the press correspondents and Tinsey concocted a
pernicious drink out of rum, whisky and red wine which laid us all
flat by midnight.

December 17th

Our turn for standing patrols over the airfield which meant a rest
for the section leaders and myself, which was just as well, as I had
collected the most fearful hangover from the previous night's
indulgences. Busied myself with my squadron administration duties
which sorely needed catching up on.

Three paratroop officers dropped in to spend the evening with us.
They said that our reputation for hospitality and booze had reached
their positions in the Sejennane hills, and that they hadn't had a
drink since landing in North Africa. We very soon rectified that with
a 'Tinsey Tornado' while they regaled us with lurid stories of their
action. Their CO was a middle-aged regular who had previously
soldiered in India, and one of his subalterns told me had no more
idea of fear than he had of paratroop tactics. Having retrieved his
parachute, he would stand firm amidst the whistling enemy bullets
aimed at him, studying the terrain and twisting his moustache while
he made up his mind what to do next, which a subordinate had
tactfully to suggest. Their unit also included a doctor and padre who
accompanied them on every drop and, thereafter, went hunting for
the Hun, as a team, in a captured Italian motorcycle and sidecar.
They'd taken, so far, fifteen prisoners.

They asked me if they could 'let their hair down' if I promised to
get them back to the front line before daybreak. I promised, and
Tommy kept their glasses filled with his Tornados.

December 18th

Watched our bombers pounding away at Tunis and Bizerta all
day. Very few enemy fighters came up, and those that did, we
fought off successfully. The G/C's conference went on
interminably, after which I drank a lot of wine with 72 Squadron

boys, before setting course for home base, feeling very tired, and, for some reason, very depressed.

December 19th

Low cloud washed out all patrols, so I took the opportunity of driving up into the hills north of Souk el Arba to reconnoitre an hotel at Ain Drahaim where I intended to send my pilots for their forty-eight hours' rest period.

Jimmy and I drove like Jehu the whole way, keeping a sharp lookout for 109s which had been strafing the road earlier in the morning, which wound up into the mountains like a ribbon vanishing in to low cloud. The hotel was perched on the summit, and turned out to be a modern establishment with some pretty French women running it whom I reckoned would keep the boys happy.

On the way back, I looked in at Souk el Arba for a briefing, but there was nothing out of the ordinary, except that an old Harrovian W/O in 72 Squadron had turned up after being missing for two days. He had shot down a couple of Huns before being hit himself, and forced to bale out, landing on top of a Guards battalion with his old school scarf wound around his neck. The Guards commander, an old Etonian, recognised not only the scarf but a chap he'd played cricket against which called for a celebration, and the W/O's tardy return to duty.

One of the flight commanders in the Wing had gone out of his mind, and tried to take off in the middle of the night, crashing his aircraft. He was being shipped back for a rest.

December 20th

Patrolled the Pont du Fas and Tunis area escorting the Tac R planes, and kept the 109s away from them. Going to attend the evening briefing at Arba, about twenty-five FW 190s beat up the airfield but the Ack-Ack had given us plenty of warning, enough for me to park my car under some trees and find a deep ditch from which I witnessed the spectacle in comparative safety.

They scattered their bombs all over the field, and their top cover of 109s shot up our standing patrol, killing one and blinding the other in one eye, but notwithstanding, this worthy shot down his attacker with the other, a highly decorated pilot who crash-landed and died as we lifted him out of his cockpit. His aircraft proved to be the latest 109 (g) which was the first we had seen at close range, and most of it disappeared in souvenirs before the experts had time to get their hands on it for an analysis.

Peter Dunning White had just turned up with a Beaufighter squadron and got pitched into a cactus bush by a near miss. I took him back with me to spend the night at Souk el Khemis and recover from his experience. We drank and yarned about our mutual friends at home, Paddy, Janie and the bar at Tracadie which the Beaver had offered his daughter a thousand pounds to have removed, but which she never did.

December 21st

Aerodrome patrols all day, so leaving Jimmy to organise the squadron, Mac Gilmour and I grabbed a bottle of whisky from our stores and drove like Jehu up into the hills, where we arrived at the Hotel de Chênes just before lunch time. My three pilots whom I had sent up for a rest the previous day were having a whale of a time with the lady residents, and we joined them in a Bacchanalian feast washed down with gallons of champagne, which lasted until late afternoon, when we returned to our camp highly elated.

December 22nd

German reconnaissance was pretty active in the morning. An FW and Ju 88 popped out of the clouds within half an hour of each other, taking photos of the aerodrome. They got a pretty hot reception from the flak, and shrapnel was flying everywhere. Monty Falls let fly with his captured German machine gun which had been given him by the paratroops, and we saw his tracers going straight into the belly of the Junkers.

In the afternoon, we patrolled the road between Tebousouk and Mejez, while the army were very busy running up their supplies to the front line. Everything looked fairly peaceful on the ground, and we didn't see any enemy aircraft. On the way back, the Americans opened up at us over Khemis, and shot down one of my boys.

Jimmy took some of the boys over to see him in hospital, and he seemed quite cheerful. He had been shot in the rectum with a 50 cal bullet, and was lying on his stomach awaiting an operation to remove the slug.

December 23rd

Low cloud and rain covered the airfield. We remained at

readiness all day, for an impending show, huddled around a smoky fire, while the rain soaked into our tent and turned the soil under our feet into a quagmire.

Sheep Gilroy tried to persuade me to take to the air on a ground strafing mission, but I stalled on account of the unserviceability of my Spitfires and the airstrip, knowing damn well that the weather would make the sortie abortive, in any event. He persuaded 93 Squadron to go along with him instead, but had to give up the project as a very bad deal.

In the evening, we heard from the field hospital that my pilot had died on the operating table, and I blew my top. I determined to hold an investigation, and told our Doc to go over to the hospital, first thing in the morning, and bring back a damn good explanation from the surgeons, or else. What else, I hadn't figured out, so the Doc poured me a very stiff whisky and told me to cool it.

December 24th

The day before Christmas, the Doc told me to take a break, or bust.

Jimmy, Ivan Crawford, Dick Pertwee and myself piled into the station wagon which we had previously loaded up with extra rations and bottles of booze, and headed for the hills, leaving Mac Gilmour to cope with the rest of the squadron. We were the only members who had, so far, not spent a night out at the Hotel de Chênes.

I drove like the wind, while Ivan sat top cover on the roof spotting for enemy fighter bombers in order to give us fair warning to hit the ditch. On our arrival, we found that the guests and management had made a gallant effort to improvise the place with a Christmas atmosphere. Decorations hung from the ceilings and walls, and the top of a fir tree towered precariously in the corner of the dining room. Half a dozen of the younger and more enthusiastic lady residents and staff were busy decorating it with tinsel and gewgaws, squeaking with delight at their efforts, while the menfolk sat quietly smoking and sipping their cocktails.

The war correspondents Guy Ramsay and Bill Mundy ordered a bottle of Dubonnet to go with a bottle of gin Ivan had produced from his flying jacket pocket, and we settled down to stimulate an appetite and Christmas spirit for peace and goodwill to all men, hoping that our enemy was doing the same thing. We had an excellent dinner, washed down with gallons of champagne and the

party continued well on into Christmas morning, while the boys
sung non Christmas squadron songs such as the 'The Ball of
Kirriemuir' and the 'Harlot of Jerusalem' to the delight of the
French ladies who couldn't speak English.

On reaching my bed, at last, I found myself unable to sleep, as
my brain started to girt in a maelstrom of memories. As Jimmy had
said, it was not the air combat that was getting us down, but the
continual movement from place to place, the chaotic organization,
the anxiety of a sudden German counter offensive, and the ceaseless
attacks, night and day, by bombs and machine gun fire. There was
never a moment to let up. When one was not seeking the enemy in
the sky, one was ducking his bullets on the ground. I had found
myself incapable of a full night's sleep, as I tossed around my plans
and new tactics for the morrow, worrying about my young pilots, the
condition of the deteriorating landing strip and the whine of a
Daimler Benz engine approaching overhead.

At my last briefing I had been told that in the event of the
possibility of our airstrip being endangered by a counter-attack and
capture, the pilots were to put their mechanics into sacks, rope
them to the wing roots, and fly them out with the aircraft. As a one
time Supermarine test pilot, I had determined that, should the
occasion arrive, I would disobey my instructions, even if it meant
my court-martial, since this action, I was convinced, would most
certainly lead to catastrophe.

I was drinking to extremes, I was fully aware of, but it brought
the only relaxation I ever got, and without this I would have blown
my fuse. I compared this life with the trials of Dunkirk, the Battle of
Britain and the relentless sweeps over the cold North Sea into
occupied Europe, listening all the while to the throb of one's single
engine, for it to falter and bring you down to a death by freezing.

This, I had opted out of, run away from, perhaps, I didn't know
which, for an alternative of fighting over my own territory where
sudden death superseded the alternative of slow drowning, or
imprisonment which I feared more. It now seemed that my
Nemesis had caught up with me. In those days, I hadn't witnessed
so graphically the death and destruction I now knew so well, and I
was younger, able to forget, and able to sleep in the arms of
someone I loved.

On this Christmas eve, I had suddenly grown old and tired but I
couldn't sleep. Closing my eyes, I tried to imagine that I was back in

England, the squadron released after a battle over Northern France, and I was lying on the perimeter of the airfield. High summer, and the larks disturbed by my presence, hovering and twittering, as I lay listening for the six o'clock chime from the little village church in the valley to signal opening time in the neighbourhood pub, at which time I would stroll leisurely down the bridle path to rendezvous with the boys and their girls…and my girl.

I remembered what she meant to me in those dark and frightening days. Besides sexuality, she had been young love in all dimensions but I knew that this would now be changed, as this bloody war had changed my mentality, irrevocably. I had grown up, matured in the hard terrain that grew the grapes of wrath from which was made the Algerian wine which fired dying embers.

I remembered how she greeted me, returning from desperate sorties, thirty thousand feet and alone above the earth, and when I was happy to be alive, which now I sometimes thought I was no longer. The little inn, so cosy and unrealistic in my world of conflict, and a temporary refuge only, I knew, but one essential to my survival, as was the body of my beautiful young lover, whom I knew I would grow out of, on this Christmas morn of 1942 in the mountains of Tunisia.

I knew instinctively that if I survived this battle, I would not go back to where I had been before, to whom I'd loved before, my first and only love that I had taken advantage of, maybe, because of her pity for me. That I must go on to some other sphere of action, some other conflict, with no strings attached, except those entwined in the silk of my parachute. This was my destiny, until the world was at peace once more.

But I also knew that I could never forget her.

Christmas Day, 1942: Hotel de Chênes

The previous night's celebrations accounted for that certain pain between the eyes as I staggered out of bed, bathed and shaved, then made my way gingerly down the stairs to find the rest of the boys already seated around our last bottle of gin. We had promised to go down and drink a toast with our friends of the Press in Ain Draham before lunching back at the hotel. The tortuous curves of the road were circumnavigated more by good luck than good judgement, and the faithful Humber deposited us back in time for our Christmas dinner.

The weather had cleared, and one could see down the mountainside where the road twisted away into the distant valley of Souk el Arba. It seemed a different world down there of sad memories, conflict and bloodshed. High up on this mountain peak, I felt security for the first time since landing in North Africa. An atmosphere of peace pervaded our little hostel, and as I looked down upon that other world, I shuddered at my thoughts of the valley of death and destruction.

This evening, I would be back amongst it all. Running the gauntlet of enemy fighters, ever present, ever seeking to destroy. I felt more tired this Christmas than I thought any man could ever feel. Living on my nerves and alcohol, I hated that valley more than I had hated any place, and wondered whether my Nemesis would catch up with me down there.

I had been trying to do too much. To live up to the standards my pilots expected of me, and the faith they seemed to have in me. I could see the red light ahead, but I dared not let anyone know. It was going to be my biggest battle, trying to defeat the growing fear, and deadly weariness. I think Jimmy knew my feelings. I sometimes thought he knew me better than I knew myself.

I wondered what my family were doing. Where Paula was celebrating, and with whom. Whether they thought they'd ever see me again. I doubted that they would.

Behind me, I heard Jimmy telling me to 'Snap out of it, Sir. The boys are waiting for you.'

I wished he wouldn't always call me, Sir. It put an unwanted barrier between us. I desperately wanted someone who would tell me what to do. Jimmy was five years older than me, but hadn't had the fighting experience I had, so it was me to give the orders, make all decisions upon which the lives of all of us depended.

I could now see the difference between those battle of Britain days and now. Those days when I was just a carefree and irresponsible young pilot officer who took orders from his CO and let him do all the worrying. It was so much easier to take orders than to give them. It was my responsibility I felt for my pilots, much less experienced than myself, that made me lead every squadron mission, although I knew my mind and body wouldn't stand the strain much longer. But what else could I do when I knew that Jimmy couldn't see the enemy fighters at the distance I could, and Mac Gilmour had never quite recovered from his crash landing.

The boys expected me, and only me to lead them. Keep them out of trouble. Somehow, they regarded me as their lucky mascot, and I just had to keep going until I cracked. Alcohol had become my panacea. Those long warming draughts that made my adrenalin pump, anaesthetised my fear of defeat, and let me sleep throughout the nights of bombardment.

Jimmy interrupted my thoughts once more: 'Come on Sir, we have a guest for lunch and the boys will be ravenous.'

We entered the warm, jovial atmosphere of log fires, decorations, popping champagne corks and laughter. This was Christmas, and Christmas we would celebrate, come what may.

Our guest proved to be Andre Levey, the French millionaire owner of Monoprix stores. He had already become acquainted with the boys, and seemed to have an understanding of their actions. However, he didn't seem to enjoy himself as much as we did, and at the end of luncheon, asked us quietly if we would drink a toast with him, to his son who had been killed last Christmas day, fighting with an RAF squadron over Malta. We did, and thereafter he left the table with tears in his eyes, and no one tried to interrupt his departure.

How we ever got back to Souk el Khemis, I shall never know. I vaguely recollect a most hazardous journey, during which another bottle of brandy was consumed, a French lorry run into a ditch and an encounter with an enraged signal corps man who claimed that someone had shot away the communication wires he had just laid to our control tower.

When we arrived back at our camp, I discovered that we had added another member to our party in the shape of a diminutive Welsh private whom one of the boys had discovered in the hills. Diffidently, he confessed that his only claim to fame was that he was undisputed champion spoon castanet player of South Wales. We put him to work at once, to the accompaniment of our only six gramophone records, and he bashed away on our spoons until passing out through drink and exhaustion.

Before the evening had drawn to its close, the officers had called on the sergeants' and airmen's messes to share in their celebrations, and in turn, most of the NCOs wound up in ours to drink to each other's health and happiness despite the bombs, the bullets and the bloody rain.

December 26th

The rain continued to pour down all day, bogging down our Spitfires up to their axles, and turning the landing field into a bog. In a desperate effort to keep the strip serviceable, the engineers had placed rushes under the wire meshing to prevent it sinking into the mud.

This might have proved a good idea, but, in effect, every time an aircraft took off, the rain was squeezed out of it, like a wet sponge, and diluted the carburettor with water resulting in motor failure. A further hazard was that the strip was so narrow that the slightest swing on take-off could take a plane over the edge, into the quagmire, and onto its nose.

In the evening, Jimmy and I called on *Monsieur le fermier* more in hopes of seeing his pretty daughter than being sociable, and in our conversation, he mentioned that it was a great pity we had not laid our strip on the field the other side of the road where the sub-soil was sand which filtered the rain.

We thanked him for this somewhat belated information, and drove over to investigate this possibility of a new landing field, and sure enough, the ground he had mentioned was firm under foot, and unaffected by rain.

I told Ronnie Lees of our discovery at the evening conference, and he said he'd get the engineers to investigate the possibilities of a new strip as soon as possible.

December 27th

In the morning, a Ju 88 and a FW 190 flew over the airfield taking photos. One felt horribly naked and unprotected without an inch of cover except slit trenches filled with water. However, we all decided it was better to risk drowning than a 20 mm slug in the guts.

In the evening we managed to get off the ground to do a patrol over the Pont du Fas area. It was a sickening sight to see the Spitfires aquaplaning down the strip, swerving and ducking like speedboats with the spray flying up in their wake.

On our way home, we saw clouds of smoke rising over Khemis, and we knew that the Huns had revisited us in our absence. Nobby Clarke's engine gave up the unequal struggle against water in the carburettor, and cut dead over the mountains. However, he managed to put it down in one piece, and wandered back to the airfield the next day.

December 28th

The army was having a pitched battle around Pont du Fas, and asked us to go over and shoot up the eight wheeled, self-propelled enemy guns that were causing a lot of trouble.

As we were walking out to our aircraft, the enemy came over in force, and I yelled to the boys to hit the slit trenches, and dived into the nearest one by yards. I lay in this, half under water, and watched them as they proceeded to shoot down the standing patrol over Souk el Arba, then bomb and machine-gun the field. The patrol didn't seem to have been given any warning of the attack, and having put up a gallant fight against overwhelming odds, first one and then the other spun down enveloped in flames to crash into the hillside carrying their pilots with them.

As soon as the Huns had left the area, we dashed out to our Spitfires and rendezvoused with some Hurribombers over Pont du Fas at the same time as a formation of Ju 88s heavily escorted by 109s appeared.

I led the squadron in behind the Messerschmitts, and blew up their leader with my first burst, before attaching myself to his wing man who must have been a novice as he took little evasive action, and notwithstanding my cannons jamming, I peppered him with my two machine guns from minimal range until my de Wilde set him on fire.

He struggled into cloud cover where I lost him, and maybe he eventually got home, but I thought more likely, as the boys did, that he joined his leader in the mountains below. They had got some good time in on the 88s, but as usual we were hopelessly outnumbered by the superior forces mounted against us from Sicily and Sardinia.

Without cannons, there was no point in looking for the target we were assigned to, and I cursed my armourers although I knew it was the rain's fault rather than theirs that they had jammed. As I circled the airstrip preparatory to landing, I watched two Hurribombers and two of my boys swing off the runway and crash onto their noses.

I saw Jimmy's tail wheel had been torn off on take-off, so told him to land at el Arba so as not to make our field into any more of a junk yard. When I had landed, I got a call to move up to a recce strip just behind the front line, and I mutinied. With Jimmy out of my way, I closeted myself in solitude and drank half a bottle of whisky, then called up the Controller to tell the G/C that I would accept no further responsibility for the safety of my pilots if we were forced to operate from where we would be sitting ducks. It was nothing but a death sentence. The Controller rang back some time later to say that my statement had not gone down very well with the Group Captain, to say the least, and he advised me to go over and see him.

By this time Jimmy had shown up, and advised me not to go in my present 'belligerent' condition, but I was determined that nothing would stop me, and drove the ten miles to el Arba at immoderate speed, with Jimmy at my side quietly warning me 'to play it cool'.

I think that I told him, then, that I had shot my bolt, and couldn't take it very much longer. It wasn't that I had become afraid in the air; today's victories had proved I could still hunt and kill with no problems, but I didn't seem to care what happened any more and, if this had any repercussions on my pilots, I'd have their blood on my hands. I don't remember much of my conversation with the Group Captain, and Jimmy did most of the talking. However, Ronnie must have realised the condition I was in, and offered me a week's leave, which I rejected.

December 29th

I felt better in the morning, and took the squadron off to fulfil the aborted mission of yesterday against the eight wheeled, self-propelled enemy guns, and didn't wait for any assistance from Hurribombers.

Jimmy told me that I'd made the attack like a man possessed, and was heading for the biggest nervous breakdown ever. He added that I'd kept him up all night fighting Huns in my sleep. I knew that his diagnosis was right, and that if I didn't accept the G/C's offer, I was for the funny farm. Jimmy had had his leg cut pretty severely during an evening raid, so I told him he was to come with me.

Group agreed to our action, and promised to rest up on the squadron during our absence, which I left in charge of Mac Gilmour. A flight of 81 moved to the strip instead, and four were shot sitting in their cockpits.

December 31st

We filled up the Humber with everything we thought we might need for our safari. Compo rations, gin, whisky, rifles and ammunition were stowed away in the back by my batman while I briefed Mac on everything I wanted done, and the boys to keep out of trouble. Especially, the members of 'The Combine'.

As we reached Souk el Arba there was an air battle going on overhead, but I kept on driving flat out, while Jimmy kept watch from the rear window for the approach of any ground strafing predator.

We sped on without stopping, until we had reached the safety of the hills beyond the target area, then pulled up, got out and relieved our mental and physical feelings. Thereafter, we ambled along the twisting mountain roads, taking in the scenery and fresh freedom air in gasps, stopping when and where we wanted to eat and drink until we reached the little whitewashed town of Guelma.

Before we were allowed to take a room at the hotel, we were told we had first to check in with the Town Major whom we tracked down to the residence of a French barrister, a charming villa in the main street. It transpired that he was a house guest, and Madame a ravishing, charming and cultured blonde. The Town Major was what one would have expected, and somewhat reluctantly, we thought, gave us a chit for a temporary residence. Madame, on the other hand, reminded us that it was New Year's Eve, and invited us to dine with her and her husband, after we had settled in at our hotel, which we gratefully accepted. The barrister proved equally charming, the dinner excellent, and the choice of wines, beyond reproach.

Towards the end of the repast, the Town Major fell asleep, and without comment, his hostess rose to place a pillow behind his head without disturbing him, as if this was par for the course. Another member of the party was a Scots doctor from the local field hospital who insisted we drank the New Year in with his Colonel at their Mess which we reluctantly agreed to, and after bidding our hosts goodnight and thanking them for their hospitality followed the garrulous Scot in a hazardous journey to a requisitioned house on the outskirts of the town where we found his Colonel fast asleep in a chair with a half empty bottle of whisky on a table by his side.

Without disturbing him, we finished his bottle before returning to our hotel at two o'clock in the morning.

January 1st, 1943

We continued on our mountainous journey, stopping where we pleased, to rest and refresh ourselves, and take desultory pot-shots at the eagles which hovered motionless in the sky above the mountain crags.

When we reached Constantine, it took my breath away. Built on the summit of a mountain, the town was divided by a ravine spanned by two bridges. Purple mountain ranges stretched as far as the eye could see, the air tasted like iced water, and the sun shone with the brilliance of a Swiss summer, reflecting a dazzling light on white villas and pensions built up in tiers along the mountain slopes. The town was seething with humanity, and pretty girls wandered along the broad pavements on the arms of their escorts.

We soon found out that there was no hotel room available in the town, but the Air Force had commandeered an evacuated maternity hospital as a pilots' transit and rest camp. We staked our claims to a couple of iron beds in a ward turned dormitory, on which army blankets were stashed and smelling long overdue at the laundry. The water was ice cold, so we decided to dine dirty.

We soon found a saloon in which to quench our thirsts and eliminate the nasty tastes in our mouths that our sleeping quarters had given us. The place was packed with British, American and French, drinking every type of liquor as fast as the waiters could serve them. I recognised several people I knew, sitting with attractive girls, obviously unhampered by differences of language. Jimmy and I must have looked a sorry spectacle dressed in our dirty battle dresses with a week's growth of beard, and were not sorry to find no vacant tables. However, an American Captain, spotting our predicament, introduced himself and shepherded us up some stairs to an ornate room which served as a senior officers' mess.

Here, we were dished a mediocre meal of compo rations, washed down with red Algerian wine, and as the room filled up, our unkempt presence drew glances of disapproval from the staff officers of First Army HQ.

We returned to the Maternity Hospital billet to find what was left of 152 Squadron celebrating. They had taken an awful beating at Souk el Arba, and been pulled out of the line for a rest. Most of them were exceedingly drunk, and insisted that we should join their party. Brandy was flowing like water, and bawdy songs floated along the corridors. When one of the pilots jumped out of a second storey window, I thought it high time to turn in.

January 2nd
We set off first thing in the morning feeling very little refreshed, and depressed at the encounter with the battle fatigued and up-tight remnants of 152. We stopped for lunch at Setif, where the French made a great fuss over Jimmy's injured leg. *'Le paurre aviateur, blessé à guerre'*, they cried. Jimmy played it well, and a splendid luncheon was produced with unlimited good white wine.

We reached the little Arab town of Boura by evening, after a wild but delightful drive through mountain passes, and along Roman roads which had never been designed for anything but horse-drawn carriages. We appeared to be the only military in the town, but a little hostel provided us with all the comforts and peace we sought.

January 3rd

We made the final stage to Algiers in fast time. As we left the towering mountains behind us, and cruised down into the plains, we could see the beautiful whitewashed city across the bay, hugging the slopes and stretching down to the water of the Mediterranean.

Our first call was at the home of Jacqueline Melz, the pretty little French girl who had helped her parents take care of Mac Gilmour after his crash three months ago. Monsieur Meltz invited Jimmy and me to stay with them, if all we wanted was peace and rest, but hurriedly added that he quite understood that there were 'other things' soldiers on leave from the front line might prefer, to what he had to offer. His clean little villa, perched up on the hillside overlooking the Mediterranean and far enough from the much bombed harbour, seemed as attractive a place as any in which to spend a quiet two days, so, since neither of us were interested in doing those 'other things' he had enigmatically referred to, we accepted his hospitality and unloaded the faithful Humber.

In the afternoon, I called in at the HQ of Eastern Air Command to discover that nobody had the slightest idea of what was going on with us at the front lines, which did not surprise me very much considering the five hundred miles of mountains which lay in between. However, they pumped me with questions about general conditions, which I answered, and they appeared at least sympathetic and appreciative of our efforts.

How the other half lived, I thought to myself as I drank a goodly number of cocktails with the Staff Officers of EAC in their luxurious mess that evening.

January 4th

I drove up to the aerodrome to see if I could find Paddy Green who had sent a note up to me at Souk el Khemis saying that he had arrived in Algiers to take over 600 Squadron. As I drove through the guardroom gates, he was the first person I ran into, and we adjourned to his office to catch up on all the news from Tracadie, the boys and

Paddy Green and myself

girls we'd left behind, and I filled him in on the news up front.

We got very drunk at lunch time, and decided to send L.M.* a letter of congratulation on his New Year's Knighthood that we had just heard about. As I was writing this epistle in rather a faltering hand, an orderly brought in a bulletin and handed it to Paddy who read it, then leisurely bought two more brandies and said, 'I see this fellow Bartley has been given a Bar to his DFC.' He tossed the document to me, and I read a list of names of pilots awarded field decorations, amongst which was mine. This definitely called for a celebration, so we agreed to rendezvous in the Aletti Bar at five o'clock and get plastered.

I can recollect very little of that evening's entertainment, except that at one time a French Algerian introduced himself to us at the bar, and insisted that one hadn't seen anything of Algiers without a visit to the Sphinx, to which Paddy, Chris Leroux and myself, all inflamed with Algerian wine, followed him. Chris was a decorated flight lieutenant from Malta. It now became apparent our guide had influence in the place, possibly a pimp, as he soon organised an

* Air Chief Marshal Sir Trafford Leigh-Mallory. Commander in Chief. Fighter Command.

'exhibition' between two lesbians in a totally mirrored room, the like of which even nauseated the tough South African who, while the two were embraced in some bizarre contortions involving a monstrous dildo, stubbed his cigarette on one of the upturned bottoms.

The scene exploded into pandemonium, more pimps burst in with drawn flick knives, and I reckoned we only survived with our balls by fighting our way out with the butt ends of our revolvers.

When we had reached the sanctuary of Paddy's jeep, he said, 'Bolshie, don't you ever breathe a word about this to Janie, or we're in real trouble.'

We woke the next morning aboard a destroyer in the Bay of Algiers, neither remembering how we got there, but as coffee was served me by a grinning but sympathetic messman, I wondered whether Chris wasn't just the man the squadron now needed. If he could fight in the air as well as he fought in the brothel I felt he was my boy, and Paddy agreed with me.

For some time, I had been feeling that Jimmy's eyesight was becoming too weak to allow him to continue operational flying, with any degree of safety for himself, or his flight, and I told this to the AOC who accepted my advice. Without a word to Jimmy, I made arrangements with Personnel to have him replaced by Chris Leroux, a South African with a sound track record.

January 7th

I had told Jimmy, on the way back, that I was having him posted, and the journey, in consequence, had not been a very happy one for either of us, but he knew my decision had been the right one for everybody's sake.

When we arrived at Khemis, we found that two more of the boys had been shot down and killed in our absence, and Mac Gilmour practically dead on his feet. The new airstrip was almost completed, and we got down to the task of choosing a suitable dispersal point, and moving our equipment to the other side of the road. It meant that we were further away from our living quarters, but I felt that our present sight was so well hidden from the air, that the men's morale would suffer if I were to move them.

Chris Leroux flew in just before dusk with a replacement Spitfire, and I introduced him to the rest of the boys and senior NCOs as we sat around our slit trench, sucking, in turn, at the rubber pipe which drew the wine from the barrel adjacent to it. I also broke to them the news of Jimmy's departure.

January 8th

It was a wet morning, and with a heavy heart, that I bade farewell to Jimmy, and watched him take off in the Caudron for Algiers. I felt I had lost my greatest friend and staunchest support. The last thing he said, before he left was that I should think about taking a rest, before it was too late. That I'd taken an awful beating from which I'd never recover if I didn't. Quit while you're ahead, he repeated, and I knew that what he said was right, but how could I?

I couldn't leave the boys until I had found them another leader who had proved himself, and whom I had initiated into all the problems which confronted us.

I knew that, next, I would have to get rid of Mac.

In the days that followed, I soon found out that in the happy-go-lucky South African, I had picked a winner. I taught him everything I'd learned the hard way, and he caught on fast, and soon became one of us without saying very much.

I sent Mac back to Algiers, and started alternating with Chris in leading the squadron on our sorties. The boys soon saw in him a leader as good or better than they thought I was, and I was happy in my choice. The new airfield was a vast improvement, and the weather seemed gradually to improve.

I was still drinking fairly heavily after the day's combat, in order to get some sleep at night, I told myself, but then I found myself taking shots during the day, to keep me going. I began to rely more and more on Chris to lead the squadron, as I felt a deadly weariness overwhelming me.

January 11th

We were drinking and listening to our five surviving records of Bing Crosby and Dinah Shore in our cottage, after a hard day's ground strafing to avenge the death of one of our sergeant pilots who had been shot through the heart in the middle of writing a letter to his mother in his tent, when we were invaded by some of the boys from 93 Squadron.

They told us they had been celebrating their liberation from hell, and were pretty well plastered. Two of them were in fancy dress, one as a Parisian dandy, and the other a whore, for what reason was unclear. On finding Chris asleep in our bedroom, the whore popped into the double bed and started to caress him.

Chris awoke with a look of amazement when he beheld this lovely creature, and like a determined batsman, started making for the crease. When he only found one stump and two balls of a young sergeant pilot, Chris grunted, 'Funny, funny', rolled over on his side, and went back to sleep.

January 12th

The army commander had told me that his opposing general had moved into a villa in the Sejennane Hills with his mistress and his staff, gave me the pinpoint location, and ordered me to destroy them. I laid on a Hurribomber for a dawn strike, and I led a section to accompany it. The bombs near missed their target but disturbed its inmates who doubled out the villa, and started running for a nearby wood for concealment. I saw a woman amongst them. They showed up clearly against the whitewashed walls, and as I made my first pass, some of them ran around the back of the house to escape my cannons and machine guns.

I followed them around as the Hurribomber got a direct hit with his second bomb. They had nowhere to run, except for the trees, and, as they did, I shot them, as I had been ordered to, and hated myself.

January 14th

We were ground-strafing some enemy gun emplacements, when attacked by some FW 190s. A huge dogfight ensued, and lead was flying in all directions, as well as aeroplanes.

I hit one, and then another, but didn't see whether I had made a kill. There wasn't time, and suddenly the sky seemed empty. Then, as suddenly, something seemed to snap in my brain. I didn't know where I was, nor what I was doing.

Two of the boys reappeared, and reformed on me, but I didn't know where I was leading them. I had lost all sense of direction. Everything seemed strange, and I burst into a cold sweat as I circled, trying to find my location.

I cursed the boys for following me with their implicit faith. Couldn't they see that I was lost. Why couldn't they find their own way home? I screamed over the RT to return to base, individually, and they left me alone, at last. I circled aimlessly, to give me time to think what had happened to me. Then, I got my bearings.

Arriving back over the landing strip, I decided I must come

straight in, without making my circuit. I had to get on the ground. Get away from my aeroplane. All aeroplanes.

I overshot twice before I judged my proper approach for a final, terrible landing.

I taxied like a madman up to my dispersal point where my worried ground crew were anxiously waiting for me, thinking that I must have been hit.

'Everything all right, Sir?' my fitter asked me as I tore off my helmet and straps, and scrambled out of my cockpit.

I didn't answer, as I staggered towards our dispersal tent, which was enough for him to realise that it definitely wasn't.

The odds against me had proved too great. Our three squadrons of obsolete Mark Spitfires against the Luftwaffe's scores of their latest 109s and 190s. Ours flying from swamp land, theirs from proper airfields in Sicily and Sardinia, backed by the radar we didn't have, the proper maintenance we couldn't get.

Something within my brain had suddenly snapped. I couldn't see anything but darkness. I wanted to be left alone.

Someone must have tipped off the squadron doc, as he showed up when I was half through a bottle of Scotch, and suggested that I should spend the night at the field hospital with him. The next morning we drove to Souk el Arba to see the G/C.

On the way, we passed two ambulances which had been strafed and burned out on the side of the road. We skidded on the fresh blood as we pulled up to see if we could give any assistance, but were told by the army team who had come to the rescue, no. All the incumbents had either been shot or burned to death on their stretchers. One driver had survived and said it was the work of 109s. Mistake, or no mistake, there was no sanctuary in this battle arena.

The interview with the G/C was prefaced by the Doc's report that I was seriously in need of a rest, and the former was most sympathetic and offered me a job on his staff. I told him that I wanted to get right away from the squadron I felt I was letting down, and he said that I was talking balls, but could take my point, and suggested three weeks' leave in the UK for which I thanked him, adding that Chris Lereux could well assume the helm of 111.

I don't know whether the G/C had assessed that I was washed up altogether, but it wasn't my intention to be. I would return, I told myself, as the Doc drove me back to Souk el Khemis.

That evening, I collected my pilots and NCOs in our cottage, and told them that I was going on home leave. I thanked them for their valiant and loyal support, and asked them to serve their new commanding officer the same, and carry on the same old spirit in my absence. I would be back, I told them, but somehow, I couldn't visualise it.

When the NCOs had gone, I told the boys I wasn't fit to lead them for a while. I was tired out, and they sang 'For he's a jolly good fellow', and we all got good and drunk. I wrote my last sortie in my Log Book. It was my three hundred and sixty-fifth combat mission.

CHAPTER NINE

Crash Landing

My batman, Cooper packed up all my belongings in my
parachute bag as his eyes filled with tears. Little Cooper, a
real gentleman's gentleman, born into his profession, he had taken
care of me, guarded me and even given me instructions to shave and
get my hair cut. A devoted slave, in whose eyes I could do no wrong.

I left in the Caudron during the afternoon, and as we circled the
airfield, I looked down at it for the last time to see the boys in their
yellow Mae Wests running out to their Spitfires on an obvious
scramble, the white cottage hidden in the woods, and Cooper waving
a white table cloth in farewell.

Those days in death's valley had seemed an eternity of mud and
weariness, and yet, I was loath to leave my squadron and my friends
who had served me so well and faithfully, and whom I was now
deserting because I had no longer the strength to face what I had left
them to. In the eyes of the public, I was a hero of Dunkirk and of the
Battle of Britain and had helped 'sweep' the skies over Northern
Europe; a double DFC and once commander of two crack fighter
squadrons. Yet, in my soul, I wondered if I was not in reality running
away. I remembered the pathetic faces of the young pilots I had seen
at the LMF Centre at Sheppey, and remembered thinking at that
time, that there but for the grace of God, perhaps my then
insensitivity, I might have been.

I met up with Jimmy who insisted I accompanied him to a show
given by some American entertainers and movie stars for the troops.
Half way through their performance, and at the first bark of an anti-
aircraft gun, the auditorium was evacuated in panic, whilst with
Jimmy I sat there thinking of my boys at Khemis drinking Algerian
wine and listening to their five remaining cracked Bing Crosby and
Dinah Shore records, in their lonely cottage. I was given a bed at the
villa of some Press Correspondents where Jimmy was staying, and
dead to the world, I fell into it.

The next few days passed in a dream while I made final
preparations for my departure to England. I took leave of the AOC

and some of the staff of Eastern Air Command who had befriended me. They made things worse by sympathy, and telling me what a good show I had put up, while I was inwardly burning with self recrimination.

January 24th

I met up with Bill Code and some others of our paratroop friends from Bône, at the Aletti Bar. Bill had been in hospital with a bad back, but was returning to the front line the following day. He told me that the 6th Commando had taken a pretty bad beating since those riotous days at our airfield, and how he had seen Peter Windsor carried down the gangway of the hospital ship crying with the pain of eight bullets in his body. He told me how tired he was, and his stammer was worse than ever.

I wandered around the city and the Casbah in a sort of daze, and lay in the sun up at the villa, bewildered at this sudden peace.

January 26th

I climbed aboard a Douglas transport plane en route for Gibraltar. We stopped off at Oran for a few hours, and I remembered that my father had told me he had once carried me up the main street when I was a little boy coming back from India. We arrived at Gibraltar in the evening as the sun was setting, a very welcome sight, bringing a strange feeling of sudden security being on British territory once again.

This time, I was billeted at the Rock Hotel.

January 27th

I fixed up my trip to England and wandered around the Rock buying silk stockings, cosmetics and local bits of jewellery for my family and Paula. I ran into a crowd of 81 Squadron who were back on rest, and to pick up the first consignment of the badly needed Mark 9 Spitfires. They said they'd had a ghastly time at Bône since we had left, and been bombed out of every hotel they had been billeted in. I lunched with Batchy Atcherley on his way through to Cairo, full of his old enthusiasm and predicting that with an Atcherley brother on either side of Rommel, the campaign would soon be over. Nobody asked me why I was on my way home.

January 29th

In the afternoon, I was warned that I would be leaving for England at midnight, and to be prepared for a call from the airfield. I was half asleep when aroused by the hall porter with a message that a car was waiting for me outside, and grabbing my parachute bag containing all my belongings, I jumped in beside the Corporal driver, and we headed for the airstrip.

When I checked in with the dispatching officer at the Control Tower, I saw two Liberators parked on the apron and silhouetted against the starlit sky. Servicemen were hurrying back and forth barking orders and delivering messages. I noticed a number of very senior officers clamped to their briefcases, talking quietly amongst themselves, and to my astonishment recognised Lord Louis Mountbatten, Admiral Sir Dudley Pound and General Ismay.

We split up into groups, and climbed aboard the Liberators. I chose the one without the 'brass hats'. As the door was being closed, four young pilots scrambled aboard with their kit bags, laughing and all very drunk. 'Nearly missed the old boat,' one giggled rather stupidly. Another told me they had come from Malta on leave after twelve months.

For some reason, we were delayed in taking off, and I could see that the crew were becoming restless. I surmised that they were afraid of being caught at first light off the west coast of France by long range fighters. Finally, we got the green light and thundered off the runway. The Rock was a blaze of twinkling lights which cast their reflections across the Bay, and I watched them from a window until we were swallowed up in total darkness.

I undid my parachute harness, put it on the bare floor as a mattress and lay down to sleep with my parachute bag as pillow. I saw the others follow my example, while the Malta pilots sat on the wooden benches and opened up bottles of booze extracted from their kit bags. I don't remember anything more until I was awakened by a shout above the engine noise, someone tugging at my arm and pointing to the window.

On looking out, I saw with horror that one of the starboard motors was on fire. At first, I tried to persuade myself and the startled company that it was only the flames from the exhaust, but soon realised our deadly peril.

The pilot barked a message on the intercom for everyone to strap on their parachutes, and for the next few minutes all was chaos as the passengers hunted for their harnesses and struggled to put them on, before a further hunt, in the semi-darkness for their packs.

For a moment I thought there would be panic amongst the navy and army men, but I was wrong. Whatever initial fears they must have had, they showed none as they followed their instructions.

I marvelled at these middle-aged military and naval men's masterful self-control in a situation foreign to them, and one in which they had been unprepared, and I read in their pale faces, the traditional discipline of great fighting professionals.

By this time the Malta boys had staggered from the toilet, and I could see were incapable of strapping on their parachutes, let alone pulling their rip-cords. When I told them our predicament, the soberest, a Canadian said: 'Aw, shit. After a year on Malta, we get fucked by Transport Command', and sat down to light a cigarette.

I scrambled up to the cockpit, and reported the situation to the pilot, a flight lieutenant and ordered him to just keep going as it was the only chance the Malta boys had, whereupon the burning engine tore away from the wing and went plummeting down towards the angry-looking Bay of Biscay, like a falling meteorite, taking the fire hazard with it. In any event, if we had been able to jump, I told myself, we wouldn't have survived the cruel sea.

First light was dawning as we held our course towards England, slowly losing height, until even as a last resort and to save some lives, a jump was out of the question. The Rubicon had been crossed, and I prayed to God that my decision had been right.

We maintained altitude on the three remaining engines, and flew on across the menacing water with fingers crossed. I stood behind the navigator who was trying to get a bearing. All radio communication had failed.

The journey home seemed interminable, until with a feeling of relief and triumph, someone shouted that he could see land ahead. Within minutes, we swept over the cliffs of Wales and spotted an airfield on our port side. How could we be so lucky, I was thinking, as the pilot altered course in its direction, at the same time lowering his undercarriage. Within moments, the other starboard engine cut and we started to lose altitude fast. Now I knew that there was nothing that could save us from a forced landing, and I shouted to my companions to brace themselves for the inevitable crash. Crouched behind the radio operator's panel, I watched the pilot straighten out, drop his flaps and make for a small field on the side of a hill, fighting the controls in a futile effort to ease our rate of descent.

I grabbed one lock of the emergency hatch, and told the radio operator to take the other and release it when I gave the order. I watched the ground rushing up to meet us, shouted my instruction and the hatch slid down the fuselage a second before we hit the ground in a nose-up power-on stall.

The tail flew off with the first impact while the rest of the Liberator turned head over heels and ground itself to pieces with its human cargo trapped inside. I recollect a fearful tearing sound of metal, a wing spar transfixing the radio operator, and a heavy blow to the middle of my back which knocked me half unconscious.

I dragged myself out of the wreckage on hands and knees as I heard the petrol splashing all around me, and the frightening noise of sizzling engines spurred me to make a superhuman effort to crawl as fast as I could away from the fire I thought inevitable.

I made about twenty yards before the pain caught up with me, and then passed out.

When I regained consciousness, I found myself in a hospital bed alongside the two pilots who miraculously seemed not badly hurt. My back was agony. I asked about the others, and they told me that a naval captain and a brigadier were on the critical list, but the Malta pilots closeted in the tail had escaped unscathed. They thought there were five dead. They were uncertain as to the cause of the fire. One thought we had been caught by a Ju 88, the other that it had been an act of sabotage.

They added that all personal communication from the area to the outside world had been stopped by a bunch of security men from Whitehall while they searched for the scattered brief cases and documents from the Casablanca Conference which the crash had scattered over the fields.

Nobody knew that I was back in England, and there was no way I could tell them. A doctor and attendant theatre sister approached my bed. He ran his hands over my battered body, asking where it hurt, and on coming to my toes, whether I could feel them. When I told him positive, he grunted I was a very lucky fellow, that the blow to my back hadn't damaged my spinal cord.

I said it bloody well hurt, none the less, and as he walked away, he gave an instruction to the sister who returned minutes later and gave me a shot of morphia which took care of everything, for how long I didn't know.

The next time I saw a face, it was a very pretty one who told me I was going for X-ray. The result showed up three broken vertebrae, and the pretty face then told me that I was going to be put in a plaster cast and that she was going to take good care of me, for which I was delighted, until she produced an enema and said, 'But first we had to empty our tum, the doctor had said', to which I replied rudely that the doc could stuff it up himself.

Later, this worthy reappeared and told me that I was being a very foolish young man, and that it was only for my relief in the embalming process. I repeated what I had told to the pretty face, and to get me another shot of morphia instead.

February 2nd

The doctor had me laid on a table with removal slats, face downwards, with nurses holding my feet and shoulders. Then, the centre slats were removed and my back bent like a bow while he bound me in swathes of plastered bandages like an Egyptian mummy.

When back in bed, and the plaster set, the pressure was unbearable, and I realised how foolish I had been in not accepting the doctor's orders. I was now completely in the hands of angel face, now armed with a syringe of morphia which she administered before I cried out with pain.

For three days I had drifted on a cloud of morphia, and on the fourth, I was on my feet, and had communicated with my parents. I was told I was bound for a rehabilitation centre at Loughborough. I kissed angel face goodbye, and told her I had fallen in love with her.

An ambulance came to pick me up, and I never asked how many of the other passengers of the Liberator had survived.

February 7th

I found the rehabilitation centre a congenial place filled with cripples like myself, and most far worse. Attached to it was a gymnasium and swimming pool for remedial purposes. The famous tennis player Dan Maskell was the officer in charge of this activity.

I discovered that the modern treatment for broken bones was to immobilise with plaster casts, then constant exercise.

February 15th

I had called Paula, finally, and she had arrived to spend a weekend in our local pub which had become accustomed to the crippled servicemen, and made them very welcome.

She told me she was still working as a model and asked me what I was going to do when I got out of Loughborough. I said I felt obligated to go back to Africa, and she started to cry. For some reason this annoyed me and I suddenly knew that we had grown irreconcilably apart because I had changed. We couldn't make love because of my plaster cage, and in my heart, I knew we never would again, but that I would always love her for what she had once meant to me. My first love, and hers.

March 2nd

They turned me loose in my plaster cast, and my first port of call was Swanbourne, with my parents. My mother didn't seem at all surprised to see me safe and fairly sound, and I remembered what she had once told me about having my horoscope drawn in the sand by an old fakir at the foot of the Himalayas when I was a baby in DarJeeling.

Strange woman, my mother, but I guess that's what two generations of India does to one. Most of the senior citizens of the village called to welcome me home, so they said, but I thought more likely to gawk at their local wounded hero, as they ignorantly took me for.

March 25th

Made my way by train to Biggin Hill, now commanded by Sailor Malan. I had called him to say that I was back, and he and Linda had asked me to stay with them in their married quarters.

Went down to the White Hart where the Prestons threw a party for me which included the twins. Cathy asked me if I had seen Paula, and all I said was 'yes'. I couldn't bend down to do up my shoelaces, and delighted in having the Station Commander tie them for me.

April 10th

Arrived down at Tracadie to stay with Janie and told her I'd met up with Paddy in Algiers for a staggering party, but didn't mention the Sphinx episode, as I had promised.

She introduced me to the fascinating Isobel who she told me was a friend of Max's and who was staying with her for a while, her permanent residence being a cottage at Cherkley.

I decided to do the same. Max had joined Sholto's staff in Cairo. I had fallen in love again.

April 25th

Went up to Loughborough for my Medical Board by train. The people in my carriage kept looking at me secretively. I knew they couldn't figure out the obesity of a body with a lean sun-tanned face, slim hips and thighs, wearing Wings and a double DFC so I rapped my chest and they got the message. A lady offered me a cigarette which I accepted and lit up, although we were in a 'non-smoker'.

When the surgeon removed my cast with what looked to me like a pair of garden shears, I felt I had lost another friend. He assured me that I was now as good as new, so I thanked and bade him farewell together with Dan Maskell and the wounded friends I had made, and caught the first train back, thinking of Isobel.

April 28th

Went up to Fighter Command for an appointment with L.M. Both he and Sholto had always made a point of 'hearing out' any of their fighter pilots whenever and as soon as we asked. On my walking into L.M.'s office, he produced my letter I had sent him from Africa, and told me 'Marshal' was spelled with one 'L'.

I told him I was as good as new, and requested a posting back to my squadron which was now in Italy. He answered he knew exactly where it was, and that I wasn't going there.

Instead, he had just the job for me training his squadrons in 83 Group, in the tactics of ground attack and army support and in preparation for the invasion of Europe. I was to report, forthwith, to Air Vice-Marshal Dickson at the Group HQ, Gatton Park, Redhill. I'd done my share of Ops.

'Right next door to your old playgrounds,' he added, 'and you can do more good for Fighter Command there than in Treble One'. I knew that he was right. I also knew that Cherkley was nearby.

May 1st

My eldest sister's birthday, and I called my parents to ask for her telephone number at Bletchley Park where I knew she worked at something to do with coding, as she spoke German, but my mother said I couldn't call her there.

My sister and I adored each other, and when she was up at Oxford at the beginning of the war I used to occasionally visit her for a party and afterwards, sneak myself, sometimes through a window to sleep it off in her room at her college. Since she had graduated and got that war job she was very vague about, she didn't confide in me any more, and I thought she had taken a lover our parents and myself would not approve of. (I wasn't to know, until war's end that her lover, and only one, was Enigma.)

May 2nd

Checked into Gatton Park and with my new AOC, Air Vice-Marshal William Dickson who introduced me to his SASO, Air Commodore Dermot Boyle, both completely different types, but splendid.

The house was a magnificent edifice fronted by Corinthian columns. It reminded me of one of the houses at Stowe. It had been requisitioned from the Colman mustard family, and stood on a hill overlooking a lake and surrounded by beautiful parkland. I was appointed one of the guest rooms all to myself, and revelled in the whole ambience after the horrors of Tunisia. Redhill aerodrome was a couple of miles away, where the Group kept its communications flight, and where a Canadian Spitfire Wing was stationed under the command of a Wing Commander MacBrien.

My brief was first, to draw up a training programme for all the Wings in the Group, for army support and ground strafing of which I had had considerable experience in North Africa. I was to use the light communication planes to get around to the airfields, and mine was a Procter.

The first time I took to the air again, I found a disturbing metamorphosis had overtaken me after the crash, and the beating I had taken in North Africa. It had left me with more than a scarred body. For the first time in my life, I found that I was afraid of flying.

I confided this to the Group medico who had become a friend of mine, and he told me that this was not an unnatural development. That my sudden fear of flying was the result of pain caused by an aeroplane, and until this memory faded and was surpassed by natural and pleasant experiences in the air, this would remain. He advised me to fly at every opportunity afforded me in my work, which I followed, but it took the best part of four months for this to take remedial effect.

Apart from my work on the airfields, I started to fly my Procter on visits to my family and friends, landing in neighbouring fields and aerodromes. Shoreham was my touch down for Tracadie, and Janie had become like another sister to me. Dear, gregarious, hospitable Janie where friends and fighter pilots were always made welcome for their snatched forty-eight hours respites from the war. On one of these, I found she had found another love who was to become her third husband. A nice Canadian army captain.

June 5th

Sailor Malan told me I should get some time in on the Mark 9 Spitfire, and lent me one of his, on my giving him my word that I wouldn't cross the Channel on a sortie.

I had a couple of double gins and tonics in the Mess before I found the courage to fly it off the ground while Sailor had a beer, and told me he had temporarily lost his nerve after the Battle of Britain, but got it back, as I would. I called in at Southampton to see the Supermarine test pilots, then flew at sea level down the south coast of England to Penzance hugging the contours of the beaches all the way. Then, on to Pembrey, for old times' sake, and to spend the evening at 92 Squadron's local pub.

June 6th

Flew back to Biggin to return Sailor's aircraft, having tried it out at 39,000 feet, and thought, if only we'd had this bird in Tunisia, I wouldn't now be where I was.

July 2nd

Week-ending at the Bull Inn at Burford with Isobel and a girl friend of hers, when Geoffrey de Havilland flew in to the nearby aerodrome at Witney where there was a de Havilland subsidiary factor. It was his birthday, and after I had introduced him to the two lovely girls he ordained that this definitely warranted a luncheon session which lasted until mid-afternoon.

Downing his last double brandy, he then insisted that we join the party he was giving that evening at the Hatfield factory, and when I asked him how the hell he expected us to get there, he replied, 'His Majesty's aircraft, naturally'.

Inflamed with wine, I thought this a most commendable solution, called the AOC's Air Attaché, and asked him to bring over his boss's Anson to pick me up. We rendezvoused at Witney airfield, and when I presented the girls as part of the package, the young officer was flabbergasted and stuttered that it was more than his career was worth to take them with us; so I told him I was pulling rank, to hop in the back and enjoy himself.

When we arrived at Hatfield, the party was in full swing, and I met up with some fighter types I knew who were surprised at my sensational company. Twenty minutes before dusk, we took off for Redhill, and on landing, were reported by Flying Control to the Commanding Officer who came roaring down from the officers' mess as we were looking for transport. He asked me what the hell I thought I was doing, and that the AOC would have my hide.

'That's only if you were to tell him, Wing Commander,' Isobel cooed after I'd introduced my passengers, and he'd taken in their looks, but fast.

'Let's get up to the Mess and have a drink,' Bill MacBrien grinned, and Isobel jumped into the staff car beside him.

As I climbed in the back with her friend, I thought over to myself what Bill had said: What the hell did I think I was doing? Whatever it was I knew that it couldn't last much longer.

During the session in the Ladies Room with Bill's squadron commanders which followed, he took me aside and warned me to cool it before I hit real trouble. I knew that I was running wild, but I didn't care any more.

August 5th

The Air Ministry had a public relations scheme in which we so-called 'fighter aces' would appear in some auditorium or other to make a plea to the long-suffering public to contribute to the Spitfire fund, before they were left in peace to enjoy what they had come to see. At the largest cinema in Croydon, this particular exhibition was being sponsored by the *Daily Express*, and the chief protagonists were to be Don Kingaby and myself. This time I had purloined the AOC's car to get there. After we had done our bit, we adjourned to the Manager's office where our hosts, management and *Express*, had laid on a drinking party for us at which Don and I got pretty high, as par for the course.

At its conclusion, I decided to pay a call at Cherkley and took off in that direction at immoderate speed. In the darkness, coming around a corner, I ran into the side of a bus approaching from the other direction, shot off the road, ploughed along a fence which absorbed most of the shock and wound up in a ditch. I could hear the infuriated shouts of the bus driver and decided that I was neither in the right place nor condition to be found, so I disembarked from the wreck, ran up the drive to the house whose fence I'd knocked down and rang the front bell.

A Dickensian matron opened the door, held up her hands in horror when she saw my face covered in blood from a cut above one eye, and hurried me inside. She assumed I had been shot down, and I didn't disillusion her. She called me a poor brave lamb and offered me a glass of milk, but I opted for some brandy for medicinal purposes, I pleaded, and she obliged me with a large one, clucking like a mother hen, which I gulped down before her door bell had rung a second time. The bus driver was accompanied by a constable and said that I was driving like a maniac drunk.

The officer asked if this were so, and I knew he could smell the truth and pointed to the empty brandy glass and bottle.

'I offered him some milk, but he said brandy would be best for him', the old duck pleaded, at which the constable suddenly winked at me, and commented that the officer knew exactly what was best for him, then offered to drive me back to my station, as my car was a write-off, he added.

We left the apoplectic bus driver repeating to the old lady that I was drunk and driving like a madman.

August 6th

A penitent squadron leader reported to his boss that he had wrecked his car on the way to visit a girl friend, and didn't deny that he had been drinking.

His boss told him that he also knew about his aeroplane and Geoffrey de Havilland's birthday party. That both were court-martial offences and to go pack his bags. He was posting him to the American Staff College, out of the country and out of harm's way.

Fighter Command took good care of its pilots.

CHAPTER TEN

A New World

October 7th, 1943

The SS *Mauritania* slid quietly out of the Clyde just before darkness fell. The sky was overcast, and the sea looked cold and menacing.

As I sat down to dinner with my four Air Force companions, I wondered whether this would prove the last meal I was going to enjoy for a while, as I noticed some of my fellow passengers looking a little green about the gills. Afterwards, I went up on deck and leaning against the railing, looked into the darkness towards the blacked-out island I was leaving behind.

I thought about its battles and its people. My family and my erstwhile lovers; in whose arms, I wondered, were they now? They were too lovely to be alone. Life too precious and impermanent. The country I had adopted and fought for, but to which I had no more claim of hereditary or birth, than my Commonwealth cousins.

The majority of the first class passengers were servicemen: naval officers going to collect new ships built in America under 'lease lend' to replace those sunk under them in merciless sea warfare; ferry pilots returning to collect yet another assignment of combat planes destined for the skies over Europe, shuttling between continents; and others like myself, on passive missions of warfare, only mine had been forced on me, to protect me from myself and my court martial.

At its maximum speed, the mighty ship ploughed through the waves, unprotected and intermittently altering its direction to avoid the predatory submarines that tried to intercept it. The monotony of life on board was only broken by eating, sleep, boat drill and ship organised concerts and quiz shows. I slept a lot, and wondered what the future held in store for me when my term of banishment was over, my transgressions buried and forgotten.

October 12th, 1943

It was an ice-cold morning when the liner pulled into Halifax with sirens blowing as if in triumph at another successful mission. Tug boats sped out to greet it, puffing importantly as they shepherded the new charge to its temporary resting place. There was neither commotion nor emotion as the passengers filed down the gangway, and made their respective ways towards the adjacent railway terminal.

So this was Canada I thought, as I humped my suitcases and looked around at the dreary dockland, the oily water and the absence of anything that looked like decent human habitation. A coloured porter took us in charge as soon as we reached the station. He checked our baggage and led us to our compartment where Duggie, Pete, Mac and I were to share a drawing room. We had just enough time to buy a newspaper and magazines before hearing the unaccustomed cries of 'all aboard'.

During our next two days of travel we saw nothing but a repetition of forests, rivers, swamps and prairie, and if it hadn't been for the colouring of the autumnal leaves and the novelty of my strange surroundings, I would have anaesthetised myself with liquor if there had been any available.

October 14th

We steamed along the banks of the St Lawrence river, beneath the towering heights of Quebec, and finally made our first halt in Montreal. We were scheduled only to stop over a few hours whilst changing trains, which was sad, as I had been looking forward to seeing something of the City and Magill University from which my brother Chris had graduated a year previously.

However, I just had time to ring his girlfriend who was exceedingly surprised to hear my voice and anxious to learn all the news from England. We started off for Washington, and over dinner decided that come what may with our movement orders, we would stop over in New York when we reached it, on the next day.

October 15th

When we arrived at seven in the morning, the room clerk at the Pennsylvania Hotel took pity on four weary British airmen and fixed us up with a large and luxurious suite which could accommodate all four of us. After a bath and room service breakfast, to the novel accompaniment of dance music and commercials, we all felt in top form once more, and determined to see as much of the town as possible.

I had been given a couple of letters of introduction, one from the managing director of Supermarines to the President of the Institute of Aeronautical Sciences, and the other by Jamie Rankin to a friend he had made on his previous visit, named Jack Leffler who ran the Broadway Piccadilly Theatre Booking Agency. I decided that the latter would prove my best bet for the fun I wanted, and called the number of his office, to be invited to make my way right over. Any friend of Jamie's was a friend of his, he added.

I found Jack in a drab little office on Broadway, standing at his desk upon which stood twenty telephones which rang constantly and simultaneously. On seeing me in the doorway, he dropped two of them, bounced around his desk and grabbed me with both hands. Thereafter, he introduced me to his partner Broadway Sam and told him to hold the fort while he took care of Jamie's friend, grabbed his hat, and bustled me through the door leaving this bedlam of noise and activity behind us.

Thence I was hurried along Broadway, through the swing doors of a garish saloon bar reverberating with music from a juke box, and a large whisky thrust into my hand. He then confided that Jamie had told him only to take water with his scotch, and asked me how he was, which I told him. As other rounds appeared and as often as I reached for my wallet, his hand restrained me.

At three o'clock, Jack suddenly remembered he had a luncheon date the other side of town, grabbed my arm and hustled me into a cab. When we reached a restaurant, we found Jack's pals had finished their lunch but were not at all surprised by his tardiness, nor his young airman protégé, whom they greeted with showbiz cordiality. After some more drinks and a hasty hamburger, his friends departed, telling Jack to take care of their tab which he appeared to accept as par for the course.

After several more saloon visits where I was introduced to more of his fraternity, my host returned to his office with me still in tow, picked up a telephone, booked me a seat for the 6.30 show at the 'Radio City Music Hall' and gave me the ticket, completely ignoring his paying and supplicating customers. Having thanked him and as I walked out the door, he shouted over the cacophony of ringing bells to meet him at Frankie and Johnnie's at nine o'clock:

'Ask anyone, he'll direct you.'

A fighter pilot was as loved on Broadway as he was in Piccadilly.

Jamie Rankin

Jack was proved right about the fame of Frankie and Johnnie's, and the first person I asked, on leaving the 'Music Hall' directed me without hesitation and with the addendum 'best hamburgers in town, kid'. When I reached the eating house Jack was ahead of me, seated at the bar next to a garrulous ex-prize fighter who was imprecating a wife he claimed had beaten him up the night before for drunk and disorderliness. Frankie and Johnnie greeted me with similar amiability and again enquired after Jamie Rankin's well-being.

More drinks taken and the famous hamburgers consumed, my indefatigable host set course for a round of the night spots of the City, and left the first one peremptorily when he couldn't get the best table on the floor which was reserved for some dignitary. Thereafter, he got what he wanted in a succession of night clubs where I drank to excess and was introduced to a number of pretty cabaret girls, finally calling it a new day at five in the morning at the Copacabana.

At midday, having checked out of my hotel, I made it to Grand Central Station and climbed aboard the train for Washington with the biggest hangover ever, and having caught up with my companions.

October 16th

Our reception at the RAF Delegation in Washington was far from cordial, and a pompous old wing commander started remonstrating on our stop over, at which Mac pulled equal rank and told him to get stuffed.

Having checked in at the Burlington Hotel where a suite had been reserved for us, we washed up and set forth to see the Capitol and the White House. The environment was one of extreme activity and bustling crowds. Automobiles charged up and down the wide boulevards as if people's lives depended upon how quickly they could get from one place to another.

As darkness fell, I was still unaccustomed to the blaze of lights in an unblacked out city, and was struck by one garish Neon sign on the top of a building which blinked 'Jesus Saves'. When I got back to our hotel, I found our suite was replete with ladies the boys were entertaining, but as none of them appealed to me, I ducked out for a snack and a movie. When I returned, I found the party over, and a legacy of empty bottles and overflowing ashtrays. I went to bed, and immediately to sleep.

October 17th

The morning was spent being interviewed by the dignitaries of the British Air Commission at their Delegation HQ. In contrast to the standards of Fighter Command, their bearing of pomposity bordered on the ludicrous. They told us that the Staff College course was virtually a waste of time, but that if we behaved ourselves as officers and gentlemen, we could prove great propaganda value amongst people who were by tradition hostile to our country. We were instructed on what topics to avoid, and to enter into no political, military nor racial argument.

I wondered from under what stones these squares had been dug up to represent us, and how different my experiences with Americans had been. We were given movement orders and tickets to proceed to the Applied School of Tactics in Orlando, to become acquainted with American technological phrases, for three weeks before continuing our assignment to the Staff College.

Having been peremptorily dismissed like a bad odour which had invaded their ivory tower, I telephoned Colonel Dean, a friend I had made in England amongst others of the Eighth Air Force (including Clark Gable) and who had been repatriated to the Pentagon, and was told to come right on over for a luncheon session, which I did. That evening, I dined with him and two nice but plain ladies, and wound up in a subdued night club which closed on the stroke of midnight. I had found Washington the complete antithesis of New York.

October 18th

During my journey south I found no traditional hostility amongst my fellow passengers that the British Air Commission had advised me of. On the contrary, they were only too anxious to introduce themselves and topics in every dimension, produced bottles of

Bourbon to share with us, and behaved generally in a typically un-English manner in their acceptance of strangers and their warmth.

October 21st

It took us three days to reach our destination during which time the warmth of the air increased as rapidly as that of our travelling companions. When the train pulled in to the station at Orlando, we found service transport and driver awaiting, which whisked us away to the Hotel Orange Court, our billet.

Given time to settle in, an officer from the School of Tactics called on us, made us welcome, provided us with a jeep and suggested that we check in with the Commanding Officer in the morning.

October 22nd

We were received with cordiality and shown around the School which we were invited to visit whenever we pleased. Alternatively, it was suggested that we might prefer to take a vacation at Daytona Beach close at hand which we decided to do. Upon returning from which I wrote my impressions to my family:

November 6th, 1943:

'We have just returned from Daytona Beach where we have spent the last week bathing, surfing and lying in the burning sun.

'We lived in bathing trunks like natives, and ate like fighting cocks. I have never felt so fit in ages. We rented a villa almost on the sands – a peach of a little place with everything from ice box to radio. Our neighbours were charming and laid on everything from motor cars to membership of the Country Club.

'The friendship and hospitality with which we are greeted by all and sundry is really fantastic. It would seem that the RAF holds a warm spot in everybody's heart.

'Tomorrow, we set out for Dallas, and from thence to the Staff College at Fort Leavenworth. This really is an amazing country. The standard of living which we have encountered is very high and runs on ultra modern lines compared to ours. Everybody drives around in enormous motor cars, and to us as strangers, one can scarcely believe that America has been in any way affected by the war yet. I am absorbing everything I see and hear, and the experience is going to be invaluable to my future outlook on life.

'Last night, we went to see an American football game between two college teams. The whole field was floodlit, and we sat there for two hours, roaring for the home side and eating peanuts. At half time, the announcer broadcast that he wished to make welcome some RAF pilots who were in the crowd watching their first game of American football. The crowd roared their applause, and we were dragged to our feet to wave to the spectators, while reporters came around asking for our names. These people are incredible. I am enjoying myself so much over here, that I sometimes get a pang of conscience when I think of the boys in England and Italy fighting their guts out.

'Well, I tried my damnedest to return to operational flying, heaven alone knows, but the powers that be flatly refused me. They told me that I was tired, that I had been fighting since Dunkirk on and off, that I had broken my back and was more use to the RAF on the ground, but I can't kid myself that I'm now not fit enough to be back fighting with the boys if I feel that I can take another tour of Ops which I do.

'Some people, I know, can't go on as long as others, but I feel that I could and should have another crack. However, there is plenty of time yet, so there's no point in worrying about it at the moment. But there's much food for thought in that quarter.

'After all, warfare is not a career one can retire from by choice, as some people are inclined to think. "He's got a couple of DFCs, why should he stick his neck out again, sort of attitude" This war is a total commitment for everyone, and no one should quit doing his job until he is either physically or mentally unable, which I am not. My conscience pricks me.'

November 18th

The Command and General Staff School is a complex of red-brick buildings in the middle of nowhere. Our nearest neighbour is the penitentiary, and whenever an execution is held, our lights dim out.

I have decided that the eight to six o'clock lecture routine is not for me – particularly after what I had been told at RAF Delegation, so I'm going to revive the problems with my back.

We are billeted in one of a row of red brick houses which used to serve as married quarters before the war. Reminds me of the similar establishment at Tangmere. There are five other British officers here, from the Eighth Army; all very decorative with medals and Cameron Highlander kilts. I can just imagine the scene they will make in

Kansas City. Michael Judd is a resident RAF instructor. Handsome chap with a very pretty wife. Resting after a tour of Ops in the Desert.

November 20th

Invited to have cocktails at the house of the Commanding General Shallenbach and his wife. Both very nice and distinguished-looking. Mrs General enchanted with the Highlanders' kilts, and a Colonel promised to have a genuine article sent her from Scotland. Another guest and student was the son of General Pershing. A shy and retiring young man who made me think of Doik Haig at Stowe. I took the opportunity of broaching the subject of my broken back, and the General was most sympathetic. None of the Americans had seen any combat, and I was granted permission to skip the first two hours of lectures to spend on physiotherapy in the unit hospital.

November 25th

My new 'modus vivendi' is not proving too onerous in my being allowed to skip the first two hours of boring lectures to lie half naked on a couch while a pretty little nurse massages my back. She says I purr like a kitten, and I wouldn't mind getting my hands on her. Naughty thoughts unbecoming to an officer and gentleman. I remembered our lecture at the RAF Delegation.

December 2nd

At another cocktail party, went to work on my General again, this time for the use of his aeroplane which he granted after the third large martini.

December 18th

Half-way through the course, and we are given a break on the 20th. Have made several weekend trips to Kansas City in the General's plane.

The Highlanders are a sensation in their kilts, as I had predicted. The local girls greet every course with the same overwhelming sensual enthusiasm, I am told, but I have decided to remain loyal to my pretty little masseuse.

December 23rd

Staying at the Colorado Springs Hotel for mid term-break. The Highlanders came with me. No snow for our anticipated skiing, so we spent our time riding around the mountain trails and ice skating. Evenings in drinking and yakking about the wars in Africa, North and West.

December 25th
Christmas Day. Rode and ice skated in the morning. Thereafter, enormous Christmas dinner with bags of booze followed by Highland Flings. Someone had dug up some bagpipes from somewhere. I think, maybe, the Colonel brought some with him from Tobruk.

I thought of my last Christmas at Souk el Khemis. What a contrast. Wondered what my boys were doing in Italy. How many were left. Still determined to get back to them, despite the ruling of L.M., but must admit my back is acting up a bit, no doubt on account of the freezing conditions outside. Miss the warmth of my pretty little nurse's hands. This has got to stop.

January 6th, 1944
Big weekend in Kansas City. The usual round of bars and night clubs, with the usual camp followers.

Breakfast wheeled in at midday on a trolley to pacify my hangover. Unsteady flight back to base in General's aircraft but made a passable landing with a Highlander in the back seat playing his bagpipes.

January 12th
Passing out exams imminent, and I a worried man on account of all the lectures I had missed in the hands of my pretty little masseuse. Cocktails with my General to whom I confide my apprehension about failing. He tells me 'Not to worry, my boy. I'll be correcting your papers personally'.

This made me feel a great deal happier, until he asked me if I would take on the job of resident instructor in the place of Michael Judd who was returning to England. I thanked him and said I'd think about it, but he knew I wouldn't. We'd grown to understand one another.

January 19th
Farewell party started in the officers' mess with the many friends I had made on the course. Previously, I had kissed my little masseuse

goodbye and promised to write her from England.

Strange how one can make great friendships in a transient life which come to a total end so abruptly. Even love.

Bade farewell to my General and his lady, and thanked him for everything he and his school had done for me. The subject of my staying on wasn't brought up again. Instinctively, he knew what next I wanted to do. He was that sort of man.

January 20th

By train through the mid-West on my way for a holiday in Los Angeles via San Francisco. What a vast and varied country this is. I think about the friends I have made and left behind: – whether I would ever meet up with any of them again – whose body my pretty little masseuse is now working over. I've got two more days of travel to do nothing but eat, sleep and think.

January 23rd

Arrived in San Francisco. A really magnificent city. Different in every way to New York and Washington. Checked into the Fairmont Hotel. Bumped into some American Marines in the bar and they invited me to join their farewell binge before posting overseas they knew not where, but suspected.

Some binge.

January 24th

By train down to Los Angeles. Sat in the Club car, sky lounge all the way, drinking gin and fresh orange juice. Fantastic views of warm drenched lands and Pacific Ocean. Forests and orange groves. I felt very sorry for the American marine friends I had made, and wished them luck.

Down-town Los Angeles where the train deposited me is a hideous place. Hot and humid. People stare at me as if I was a man from Mars. The ones that know the truth, smile at me. I hail a Yellow cab outside the station and ask for the Beverly Hills Hotel.

Stopped at a traffic light on Sunset Boulevard, the cabbie, silent up till then, stares at me in his rear view mirror, then asks if I am for real or from Central Casting. I didn't know what he was referring to. At the next traffic light, he suddenly said, 'You must be for real.' I said I was, whereupon he pulled in at the next saloon and bought us both a drink.

With 'Stevie' Stephenson and Clark Gable

I checked into the Beverly Hills Hotel where a room had been reserved for me by the RAF Delegation in Washington. I unpacked and called a number Clark Gable had given me in London. It was his home, and his secretary told me that Clark was at Metros, and she would tell him I'd called and where I was staying.

I was directed to the Polo Lounge, and a stranger bought me a drink and asked me to join his table which I did. He had taken me for real and asked me about the war in the air, of which I told him what I knew.

A couple of drinks later a waiter approached with a telephone and said there was a call for me from Clark Gable. He thought it was some joker. Clark said he'd pick me up at six o'clock and we'd take it from there. To meet him in the hotel foyer.

My new friend was nonplussed and I told him Clark was a friend from the war I'd been telling him about. He bought another round.

On the stroke of six Clark strode into the foyer, grabbed my hand and hustled me to his car parked outside, grinning all over his handsome face. He drove up to a house not far from the hotel, in Beverly Hills. He told me it was the home of one of the studio's Vice Presidents, an Irishman like me, and a good friend of his.

I was introduced to Eddie Mannix, his wife who went by her stage name of Toni Lanier, Betty Hutton and Kay Williams whom I gathered was his current girlfriend.

After a few strong whiskies, Clark said he had to leave me, but grinned, 'in very good hands', and to come out to Metros in the morning where he was working on a documentary. Kay Williams left with him. Toni Lanier said the rest of us would go on to Romanoffs for more drinks and dinner. We all piled into her car, and I sat in the back with Betty Hutton. Toni sang all the way there. Betty, I thought, was the cutest thing I'd met since Paula.

Prince Michael Romanoff greeted me effusively in an old Etonian accent, and the first round was on the house. Toni whispered in my ear that he was in reality an East End Jew.

After dinner, Eddie said he was walking home, and Toni that the rest of us were going on to the Mocambo, which we did. She ordered champagne, and I danced in turn with both the ladies. Betty was looking cuter every moment, and Toni drunker. She whispered she'd like a piece of me, and how about it, some time. I pretended I didn't know what she meant, and just said 'thank you' which seemed to satisfy. Meanwhile, I was falling in love with Betty Hutton. A photographer came to our table and took some pictures. Toni told him I was a fighter ace and buddy of Clark Gable. I knew it was time to leave, and that I would drive the car.

February 5th
Toni Lanier called me in the morning to say she'd drive me out to Metros to meet up with Clark and show me around. I could do nothing but accept, and within half an hour she showed up looking none the worse for wear. We found Clark busy in a cutting room on his picture and happy, I felt sure, for someone else, less preoccupied to show me around. We visited sound stage after sound stage, and she introduced me to Mickey Rooney and Liz Taylor.

We wound up the tour on a vast stage where a musical was being shot, and she told me I could take my pick of the chorus girls should I fancy that action. I declined. We lunched in the Commissary where I saw and met famous faces who happened to come by. Obviously, one couldn't pass by Toni Lanier's table without stopping to say 'hello'. Checked in with Clark before we left who said 'same time, same place'. That evening was a repetition of the previous.

February 6th
Nigel Bruce had called and asked me to drinks at his home that evening. He was well known to extend similar hospitality to any visiting British service personnel, I had been told.

Again I found the house was one of a row on Beverly Drive, and wondered why most of the wealthiest people in Hollywood lived practically on top of one another. I could not possibly have recognised him as anyone else but Doctor Watson, and his wife was charming. Liking what he saw of me, apparently, he said they were taking me on to a cocktail party at the Basil Rathbones whom I subsequently found out to be the social lions of the British Colony. On meeting the famed Sherlock Holmes, he hissed an aside to me, 'For God's sake behave like an officer and gentleman in this town, and don't you let the side down, old chap.'

Their entire conversation revolved around themselves and after one insipid drink, I excused myself and made my way to the Mannix's and thereafter to Betty Hutton's apartment, as we had planned.

A telegram arrived from the British Air Commission to report back to Washington immediately. Eddie Mannix collected the friends I had made for a farewell party at his house. Clark brought Kay Williams. I brought Betty Hutton. We dined at Romanoffs, then Betty and I went on to the Mocambo alone.

Back in Washington, I was told I had been assigned as an instructor to the School of Air Tactics in Orlando, and to report to Wing Commander Donaldson. I remonstrated against this unexpected detention in the United States in an instructor capacity which I had had enough of already. I knew that the big day was coming and wanted to be there on time.

February 8th

I checked into the School of Air Tactics, dumped my kit in a wooden frame house on the edge of Dubsdred Country Club where I was to be billeted, and met Teddy Donaldson. Teddy's reputation as an aviator was legendary throughout the United States Air Force, from coast to coast. He flew a hotted-up Airocobra which he had stripped for lightness and manoeuvrability, and after a couple of American fighter aces had tried to emulate his aerobatics (not knowing about his modifications) and been killed he had been warned to 'cool it', in future.

The Officers' Club was running short on its whisky and gin ration, and the Club secretary approached me to use my diplomatic passport to fly him to Nassau where he assured me we would replenish the supplies. To uphold the honour of the RAF I could hardly refuse, and the Commanding Officer's B.25 was put at my disposal.

When I checked into the RAF Mess, Nassau, I was told that, unfortunately, the supply ship they were expecting had been torpedoed, so they were short themselves, but that in Havana the supply of liquor was unlimited. I hoped that my diplomatic privileges extended to Cuba and headed on south.

The information was correct and we bought 75 cases, which we took to our hotel in a hired truck. Our mission accomplished, we decided to see the town, and got picked up by a pimp in an open-air night club. He suggested a whore house of some repute, but I declined. Having seen an 'exhibition' at the infamous Sphinx in Algiers, one's seen the lot. I left my crew to indulge themselves, and started back for the hotel, when the pimp said he would accompany me. I replied it wasn't necessary, but he insisted. He suggested another place even more erotic, but I said I was going to bed. When we entered the hotel lobby he said: 'You would get into big trouble if I told the police you were smuggling liquor, so let's talk it over at this place I know. It's just near here, what do you say?'

'OK' I said, 'let's walk.'

We started down the drive between the palm trees and when we were out of sight of the hotel, I hit him behind the ear with my ·38. He went down like a ten pin and I dragged him off the road behind a tree. I went back to the hotel and double-locked my bedroom door.

The next morning we were up at dawn and piled into the truck on top of the liquor. As we passed the spot where I left the pimp, I was relieved to see that he had disappeared.

While loading up the crates we got our weights and balances wrong, the B.25 tipped backwards on its tail, and soon after some liquor started leaking from it, which attracted considerable and suspicious attention from the Control Tower. Having hastily rectified this indiscretion and the aircraft's equilibrium, I checked in with the Tower to file my clearance, and, to throw them off my trail, I decided on destination Nassau. We staggered off the ground and when a long way out of sight, I altered course for Florida. To confuse matters further, I had decided to touch down in Miami which I did, and taxied directly over to the Air Force maintenance depot, across the field from Civil Flying Control.

I figured they would assume it was our proper destination, but the depot's commanding officer knew it wasn't and asked what the hell we thought we were doing. One of the crew handed out a case of Scotch, the CO got our message, grinned and said he'd clear us with the Control Tower, whereupon we took off again for Orlando.

A truck was waiting at dispersal to off-load our loot, and by the time it took for Customs and Excise to catch up with us, the B.25 was empty. They had tracked us all the way from Cuba. In the

Officer's Club, thereafter, the General bought the drinks, and we all shook hands, after a case of Scotch and one of gin had been deposited in Customs and Excise's car.

March 5th
'Dearest family,

'I'm being kept on here against my will for some strange reason, I know not. If I miss out on the invasion, I'll not forgive the Royal Air Force, and by that I mean those pompous chaps in Washington. I give a few lectures on air fighting in respect to army support which I learned in Africa, or tried to.

'Otherwise, I just laze around in the sun, ride, swim, play golf and drink too much. Most frustrating, but today I got my hands on a Spitfire and showed the fellows how it really worked. I think even ace Teddy Donaldson was impressed.

'I was down in Nassau and Cuba the other day, but the less said about that the better in case I'm censored. Le Prince de Galle and Simpson not so popular and unsociable, on all accounts. Glad I got my two DFCs from his brother, and you, your Knighthood, Pop. My General hints I have something more interesting than running liquor coming up for me on the West Coast, but won't say more.

'At least, it will give a chance to resume my romance with you know who, but I read somewhere that Clark had taken her over. Such is a miserable life.'

March 10th
Took off for Los Angeles in the B.25, second piloting. No mission stipulated. Very odd, and I don't ask questions, as I feel I wouldn't get answered. So be it, but I hope to meet up with Betty at least. Refuelled at Dallas and El Paso, and landed late evening in L.A. Spent night at Air Force Base.

March 11th
Flew in to a godforsaken airstrip in some godforsaken desert far north east of L.A. All quonset huts and cacti. We were greeted by a strange bunch of air force and some 'boffins'. Can't figure out what our scenario is. None of us can, but we are told we will be carrying out some tests over the next few days.

March 12th
When we got out to our B.25 we found it surrounded by Air

Force and boffins examining an egg-shaped bomb with an overlarge set of tail fins which reposed in its cradle. A brigadier general said that he wanted some aerodynamic tests done and then produced a map which indicated the bombing range. He added that it was a prototype of an anti-personnel missile. The ground crew bombed up, various bods climbed aboard and we got airborne under the General's command.

Having reached the altitude he wanted, we made our run up, and let the egg go on target. The General seemed pleased with our airmanship, and said we'd repeat the performance the following day.

When I asked him what the bomb was designed for, he told me anti-personnel again.

My Colonel co-pilot's comments were, 'Anti-personnel, my ass. These Dodos have laid something extra special, is my guess.'

'Like poison gas?' I suggested.

'Can't think of nothing else,' he added. 'But they ain't telling, for sure.' So, we left it at that.*

It appeared to fall much slower than the ones that near-missed me in Tunisia, due to the very large fins, but everyone seemed pleased with our tests, and we were told to return to L.A. in the morning.

Orders changed before take off. Fly direct back to Orlando, only stopping to refuel, same places. Funny-looking bomb, I kept thinking. Seem they want to get rid of us fastest. 'Looks like they're playing dirty pool,' my co-pilot said. So back to Orlando we go, and report in. Our Commanding General gives us a quizzical look, and we wonder what he knew about our assignment we didn't.

Abruptly he tells me he has my orders to report back to Washington, and that air transport had been laid on for tomorrow. Farewell drinking party in the Officers' Club, with my imported drink, and with the friends I had made. Once more wonder whether I will ever see any of them again. Funny, funny life it is.

April 13th

Queen Elizabeth loaded to the gunnels with 15,000 troops, I've been told, and definitely top heavy, I feel. What a target for any sub which could catch us, but we jink like crazy.

---

* And that was that until after the war when I saw a replica in a museum, and from my discussions with American top brass over date, and place, it seems certain that this was 'It.'

CHAPTER ELEVEN

Operation Overlord

April 20th

Everyone talking about the invasion when I reported in to HQ
Fighter Command. Head of Personnel told me there was not
a hope in hell in getting back on Ops, and there was no point on
trying to work on L.M. He wasn't having any. Too many of the 'Few'
had got the chop, and three tours was 'it' as far as I was concerned. I
was being posted to the 70th Fighter Wing of the American Ninth Air
Force to put my US indoctrination to good purpose. I was to be on
their Staff as one of their A3s, and more important, liaison with the
RAF. He didn't even give the chance to get at LM.

I had already contacted family and friends to find out how and
where everyone was placed before the 'great day'.

May 1st

Checked into HQ 70th Fighter Wing and with its Commanding
Officer, Brigadier General Macaulay, a spruce and very military
looking gentleman from Maryland who was interested in horses. The
Wing flew Thunderbolts stationed around Middle Wallop.

May 5th

Checked in with Jamie, commanding an 83 Group Wing at
Biggin. I was all set for air transportation with an L.4 provided by
the Americans to get around their squadrons and meet the chaps, but
I had no ground transport that I could use ex-officio, and Jamie
suggested the twins' SS 100 which had been laid up for the lack of a
petrol supply since Brian had gone to Italy.

Rendezvoused at the White Hart, Brasted, for a party weekend.

May 6th

Twins said I could borrow their SS, and Jamie sent me packing
back to work with a full tank. My General gave me chit authorising
me to refuel at any American Army or Air Force base, so that
problem was solved.

May 10th

To Shoreham. Janie picked me up in the Railton for a Tracadie weekend. Cynthia is staying with her, looking prettier than ever despite her busted arm which she says she will never get the proper use of again. Poor lovely Cynthia.

I think I've fallen in love again.

May 16th

Checked into East Leigh to whoop it up with the Supermarine test pilots. Jeffrey Quill told me that Geoff Wedgewood had been killed commanding 92 in Malta, and George Pickering in a motor car accident. How ironic for the great test pilot he had been.

The Clausentum Club will never be the same again.

Geoffrey Wedgewood

May 28th

Orders to get myself down to Southampton pronto. The 70th HQ unit was on its way in the morning. The balloon is obviously about to go up.

Roads barricaded off to the south except for Army transport.

May 29th

Sail leisurely down in the SS 100. No roads barred to me with the movement orders I carry, but inquisitive looks at my racing car, now repainted air force blue, and the squadron leader dressed in American battle dress behind the wheel.

Stopped to tank up to the full at an American petrol depot, before garaging it, as I proposed, at Supermarines whilst across the Channel.

May 30th

Southampton buzzing like a bee hive. MP Posts and road blocks everywhere. I asked for Ninth Air Force bivouac area and was directed to the main road running east from the town to Fareham which I had travelled many times in the past, now barely recognisable.

South of this was cordoned off with barbed wire fencing behind which were hundreds of tents. The line of fencing was broken intermittently by sentry huts guarding entrances. I located the Ninth Air Force bivouac, by its notice board...*then, suddenly, I saw my brother.* He was walking up the road looking for his location, obviously, and in the battle dress of the Royal Army Medical Corps. One was as surprised as the other. He jumped into the SS with his kit bag, I made a fast 'U' turn and drove to the Clausentum Club. George Pickering's wife behind the bar. I offered my condolences about poor dead George, introduced Chris, and she poured three large whiskies.

I made arrangements for the storing of the SS at Supermarines which George's wife said she'd take care of.

Chris and I caught up on everything that had happened to us since we last saw each other six months previously. The drinks continued to be on the house. We drank to poor dead George until closing time. When Chris and I decided to take off up to Swanbourne to surprise visit the family before incarceration behind the wires. Quite crazy, but what the hell. We didn't know when we'd get the next chance to see them. Returning next morning we parked the car and checked in.

George Pickering

June 2nd

Incarceration was getting me down, particularly with the thoughts of the Clausentum Club and my Supermarine friends just up the road, so I thought up a ruse to get me out from behind the wire. I told my General that I carried a ·38 with only one load, not the US standard ·45, and that I should get more ammunition from the British sector. He agreed, with a wink, and gave me a pass to get out.

Made my way to the Clausentum Club, had a drink with George's wife, retrieved the keys of the SS 100, and high-tailed it for the pub George and I used to patronise, near one of our dispersed assembly plants and airstrips.

As I walked up to the bar, first person I saw was Sheemy Lovat, drinking with his Commando officers. He asked me what the hell I was doing outside the wire, and I told him I suffered from claustrophobia, and how about him. He said he suffered from the same thing, and bought me my first drink of many. I made it back to the Club, and thereafter my stockade, just before curfew, and feeling very much happier. I'd swapped my ·38 for a ·45 with one of the guards.

June 5th

Noise of aircraft overhead, all night long, and we knew that the invasion was on at last.

June 6th

We piled aboard lorries which conveyed us to the docklands where we scrambled aboard one of many landing craft. When full to capacity, it took off down the Solent, the sea getting choppy as we headed out into the Channel. Luckily I'm a good sailor. Others weren't.

Cut between two battle wagons whose guns are pounding the beachhead. Bloody awful noise of screaming shells and bangs. Looked like thousands of aircraft streaming over head, many towing gliders. I'd been told to wear a steel hat, and carry a rifle. Except for my wings, I was indistinguishable from the rest, and felt a proper Charlie, but consoled myself that I had my old Stoic tie in my pocket which I planned to put on as soon as we hit the beachhead.

We hit it with a sudden lurch. I dropped my rifle as I jumped into the surf, and didn't bother to retrieve it. The beachhead was littered with wreckage, and white boundary tapes showed us the way to go between the minefields.

Single-filed up a path to the top of the beachhead. Saw dead cattle everywhere, hit by shell splinters, bloated, fly ridden and smelling to high Heaven. Also, some dead Krauts in machine gun nests. Our dead must have had a quick burial, as I saw none.

Found a farmhouse and barns which we took over. Local inhabitants in shock. We were told to dig ourselves in, in surrounding fields. Picks and shovels made available by airstrip construction commandos. When I'd dug my trench, I found a barrel of cider in a barn, and set to celebrate.

June 8th

Noisy night, but slept through most of it on account of some calvados someone had found. Lethal stuff, but tranquillising. Some fanatical young Hitlerites who had refused to retreat with their comrades were holed up in surrounding haystacks and camouflaged trenches from whence they sniped at us, which angered the American Rangers who had spearheaded our landing.

I watched them smoking, meditatively, in their half-tracks, seemingly impervious to the intermittent bullets which whistled around us. Then, their sergeant stubbed out his cigarette and said, 'Let's go, fellows', whereupon four half-tracks roared into action, and took off across the fields in the direction the firing was coming from, fanning out as they proceeded. I watched them through my field glasses I had taken off a dead Kraut, as they attacked from four points of the compass, converging on the nests, in turn, machine guns blazing. When they reached them, they spun around on top, grinding the survivors of their bullets to pulp, my inspection later showed.

Then they roared back to their starting point, cut their motors, and produced the ubiquitous pack of Camels to light up again, while they discussed the latest baseball scores they had heard on the Voice of America.

June 14th

Relaxing in my slit trench drinking cider out of a petrol can when interrupted by a breathless flight mechanic who said he had spotted a Spitfire which had landed in a field between us and the enemy, and looked OK. We decided to check it out as soon as it got dark, and that we did, finishing our quest crawling on hands and knees. A cursory inspection showed nothing more the matter with it than a bullet through the glycol tank which the mechanic remedied with a stick of chewing gum, before crawling to safety once more.

June 15th

The markings on the Spitfire showed it to be one from a Polish squadron, I found out as my mechanic, now friend, refilled the cooling tank by half moonlight. Then, I flew my new baby out, and popped her safely down on our airstrip.

June 16th

My General was a little taken aback by this unique addition to his fleet of Thunderbolts, but when I pointed out its potential usefulness in my job of liaisoning with the British sector, he agreed to let me keep it, so I had the Polish marking removed and the letters A.C.B. to replace them. Thereafter, he decided to stable a magnificent stallion he had 'liberated' from a German cavalry unit, right next to my dispersal area.

June 17th

The German snipers had by now all been winkled out of their hidey holes by the Rangers and shot, since they refused to give up, and I had moved from my fox hole to an attic above a farm building which housed a vast barrel of red wine, and a rack of calvados, and furnished it with liberated articles which made it an agreeable beachhead 'pad'.

Flew over to the British Sector to visit Jamie Rankin, commanding a wing in 83 Group. He had just put up a notable 'black' by omitting to lower his undercarriage on landing back after a binge at Biggin and the White Hart. His ground crew told me that the alcohol fumes in the cockpit could have blown the hood off. The boys thought it a huge joke. I stayed in his caravan, carousing late into the night with him and his ALO discussing why Monty wouldn't make his move, so I could answer the question my General had been asking.

From what I could gather, the Germans feared Monty more than the Americans, and had concentrated most of their armour against his army. Furthermore, and according to the ALO Monty was a humanitarian tactician above all else, knew that the war was now in the Allied bag, and wasn't going to move his troops until the opposition had been good and truly softened up. He didn't intend to repeat a reputation of the First World War's 'Butcher' Haig, or Kitchener.

By mid-morning, my Spitfire had undergone a thorough inspection which it badly needed, and bidding Jamie a fond farewell I took off to visit Chris Leroux who was commanding a wing at a neighbour airfield. He told me that their air opposition had been slight and that on the morrow he was flying to England to celebrate his girlfriend's birthday, inviting me to come with him. We stayed up most of the night drinking red wine laced with calvados in his tent and reminiscing on Tunisian times.

By morning, low cloud had almost settled on the airfield and the Met gave us a 'diced situation report over the Channel but Chris said he was going to risk it, and started packing his suitcase. I told him it wasn't worth the risk, but he only grinned 'I didn't know his girl friend'. I couldn't stop him, and watched him take off into the gloom with his suitcase on his lap.

Thinking to myself what a bloody idiot to take the risk for a girl, some instinct prompted me to wander over to the Ops Caravan, and to my horror, over the RT loudspeaker I heard Chris calling that he was in ten tenth cloud, that his Spit had taken a buffeting and that his suitcase had broken free and was jamming his controls. Then, a series of blasphemies, followed by silence, and I suddenly realised that I had seen my friend for the last time.

What irony. What a waste of life. The war nearly won, and Chris on his fourth operational tour upon which he had insisted. The only person I knew who had. One of the most highly decorated pilots in Fighter Command, finally brought down by a dirty weekend suitcase, as he would have told it. The man I had picked to take over my squadron, after I had seen him fight in an Algiers brothel.

The last call of my British Sector reconnaissance safari was on Geoffrey Page, another friend who was commanding a Spitfire Wing flying from an airstrip near Bayeux, predominantly on ground strafing. I was badly in need of a new glycol tank as the American mechanic's chewing gum repair job was beginning to work loose, and I could trust him not to pass the word to Command on my liberated Spitfire, although I knew that its new markings of my initials on its side would sooner or later attract top brass attention.

We made a deal for his mechanics to do a regular servicing job, in exchange for which I would transport champagne and perfume in my ammunition tanks on my uninhibited visits to England for mutual disposal when leave was granted.

Previously, Geoff had been shot down in flames and spent eighteen months as a McIndoe guinea pig at East Grinstead hospital, and on release, got himself back on Ops with a vow to shoot down eighteen of his enemy. This, he succeeded in doing over Arnhem where he was caught by flak and crash-landed, wrecking his back, and putting him, finally out of combat action.

My General was pleased with my report on the British Sector, and gave me twenty-four hours' leave of absence.

June 22nd
Flew to Eastleigh to collect the SS 100 and drove it up to Northolt which I had planned as my point of departure for London town visits, and got flown back to spend the night at the Clausentum Club. I'm getting this invasion situation well under control.

June 23rd
Back to the beachhead landing strip. A bigger and better one almost completed. My General told me that he had a VIP* he wanted me to escort on a reconnaissance flight over the front lines in the morning. He would fly passenger in a two seat Mustang, with a Thunderbolt on one side and my Spit on the other, so that there would be no possible danger of mistake in aircraft recognition. The Ack-Ack boys were trigger happy, and often couldn't distinguish between friend and foe. I may say this was my idea, but my General claimed to the VIP that it was his.

I hadn't seen a German fighter around in ages, but our own Ack-Ack could prove a hazard.

July 4th
Fourth of July, and the Americans fired a salute of 1,500 guns. The British sector which I visited later said they were fired in their direction. General pleased with my British situation reports but still beefing that Monty won't get off his arse, and move.

July 14th
Went up to the front line to witness the softening up bombardment of the Saint Lô defence line by what looked like to me a thousand Forts. The wind was blowing the smoke backwards from the bomb line and subsequent waves of bombers were off loading on this, instead of target. I beat a hasty retreat to avoid getting involved. The General of the First Army got a direct hit.

---

* Eisenhower.

July 22nd

70th Fighter Wing set up HQ in German evacuated St Lô in former school house. Latrines left in appalling state. Can hardly blame the Krauts after the pounding I saw them take.

July 30th

Wing moved down to Avranches. First Army hold to allow Patton's Third to go through. He saw me coming out of a shop loaded with unwrapped bottles of wine and perfume, standing up in his jeep and with a gun on either hip. He glowered at me, but carried on at the head of his troops.

August 3rd

Germans have started to counter-attack in order to cut the US First and Third in two. My General asks me what I think he should do. Looked like we'd have to evacuate. I suggest that we call the British 83 Group's commander Air Vice-Marshal Harry Broadhurst and ask him to lay on his rocket-firing Typhoons and 20 millimetres as being far more effective than our 50 armed Thunderbolts.

Then he asked how well I knew Broadie, and I told him well enough to try him at any rate; so he bade me to get moving, which I did.

August 5th

Broadie laid on a terrific blitz on the enemy columns approaching down the road towards Avranches with his Group's Typhoons. From a thousand feet, it looked like a massacre with troops baling out, and running into the fields. The biggest traffic jam ever I did behold, for sure. The Krauts will never reach Avranches, I reckoned, and told my General so. We drank a bottle of champagne between us and added a toast to Harry Broadhurst.

August 8th

Over to Jamie's airfield to gather the latest gen from the British sector for my General, and thank Harry Broadhurst, if I saw him, for saving my skin at Avranches. Actually, I knew I would be very well airborne, before any more Krauts used our latrines. Jamie told me that Brian and Duncan Smith had turned up from Italy and made their HQ in a suite at the Berkeley, so the RAF grapevine had it, and that the grape was flowing like the Trevi Fountain. I decided to check this out forthwith.

August 11th

Flew my Spit into Northolt, my ammunition tanks, except for two, filled with Moët Chandon. After a couple of quick ones in the Mess, drove the SS 100 flat out up to the Berkeley, and found the grapevine to have been correct. Their suite was brimming with girls and barrels of Italian wine. We greeted one another affectionately, and started to catch up on everybody's news. This went on till early morn when I dossed down on a sofa to sleep it off.

Northolt Dispersal Point

August 12th

On my way back to the beachhead, I ran into a huge stream of Lancaster bombers approaching the Bayeux-Caen area at about six thousand feet, and joined in their safari. As they reached their target which I assumed were the forces opposing Monty's army, they let go their bombs and the whole ground appeared to erupt like a volcano.

August 12th

Monty had 'gotten off his arse, at last' my General told me after the evening's briefing, as he popped the cork off a magnum of Piper Heidsieck.

August 22nd

Germans in full retreat, so we saddled up and started after them on the road to Paris. Passed destruction, and the carnage on the way, caused by Broadie's Typhoons. What a massacre. I was riding in my General's jeep.

August 30th

Got as far as Versailles where we checked into the Petit Trianon.

It had been decided to let the Frogs lead the parade into Paris. *Entente cordiale*, my General told me.

September 1st

Entered Paris after the French, and drove down the Champs Elysées. Everyone waving flags at us and shouting. Predominantly girls, I noticed. 'They'll be waving their knickers tonight,' a Colonel grinned.

Heard sporadic gunfire above the shouting and were told it was the FFI knocking off collaborators.

'In American, "free from infection", and I'll bet not all the girls are,' the Colonel snickered. He'd acquired a sense of humour, I'd noticed.

The ubiquitous American Army MPs were already in evidence, halted and checked out our convoy and directed it to a Seine embankment where we parked. A wing of Spitfires suddenly appeared over the Arc de Triomphe and were greeted by a barrage of anti-aircraft fire but disregarded it as beyond contempt. As contemptible as the Free French army which led the triumphant entry into Paris.

Despite the ostentatious show of greeting, I could sense an undercurrent of guilt, apprehension and uncertainty as I had sensed in Algiers three years previously. In an attempt to demonstrate their new loyalty, collaborators were ferreted out of funk holes and publicly executed. Women, young and old, had their hair shorn to the scalp. Their German conquerors whom they had previously accepted, and who now only wanted to surrender were shot with their hands above their heads. The town felt at war with itself. Its celebration struck a false and discordant note. What was it trying to prove to its liberators, I wondered. That they had never capitulated? Never betrayed? Never collaborated? Never doubted that the Allies would win, and accepted their conquerors with minimal resistance which in a lot of cases developed into preference?

Now, they were trying to expunge a guilty conscience by turning on their brethren more guilty only than themselves in despicable and brutal ostentatious reprisal.

There was a sickness in the air, and I decided that the only healing could be found for me in the bar of the Ritz Hotel, and there I anaesthetised myself with Moët Chandon on the house.

September 3rd

70th Fighter Wing's next stop over was in Laon, but my General allowed me to bale out at Le Bourget where our L.4 had arrived already, and flew me back to Avranches to pick up my Spitfire. Flew it back to Le Bourget, and got a ride into Paris to join the festivities. Found some old chums in the Ritz Bar and celebrated, thereafter spent the night at the hotel.

September 4th

Got a ride back to Le Bourget, mounted my Spitfire with a monumental hangover, and map-read my way to Laon. Found out that the 70th was bivouacked at a spot called Marchais, not far away. Laon full of American paras who had liberated Rheims, and cases of its champagne.

I liberated an Auto Union Horche twelve-cylinder saloon from a local garage, filled the back with cases of Moët Chandon, and the tank with petrol. My voucher still worked wonders.

Tracked down the Wing HQ to the estate of the Princess of Monaco, I was told when I got there. I remembered how Rainier had run away from Stowe, and decided to call on his mother who was in residence at the Château. Put on my old Stoic tie beforehand.

She greeted me warmly when I introduced myself, and invited me to stay. She added that the officers would be welcome to a wing of her magnificent establishment. My General said, 'It's the people one knows what counts.'

September 15th

My General had decided to throw a party, and asked me to invite the Princess and she accepted. She had started calling me 'darling'.

I had started to like her a lot.

September 17th

A truckload of champagne had been collected from Rheims. At the appointed hour, I called for the Princess in her private wing. House-guesting were a distinguished French nobleman and his son. I was introduced to the Comte de Paris et son fils.

'Tony darling,' the Princess said, 'one thing I don't understand is where all the girls are coming from.' I couldn't answer this one. As we made a grand entrance down the stairs, the Princess gripped my arm and hesitated momentarily, then whispered, '*Mon Dieu. Elles sont mes domestiques et les filles du village.'*

When the party was in full swing I suddenly caught sight of the son of the Comte de Paris being confronted, it looked aggressively, by one of our senior officers who had been a shoe salesman in private life, and I moved over to the scene to hear him ask, 'Say, kid. Who's that old bugger?' nodding in the direction of the Comte. 'Is he shacking up with the Princess?', and the young man reply, 'Sir, that is my father.'

I swear I saw the portraits of the Princess's ancestors shudder on their hooks.

September 22nd

The Americans had landed in the South of France, were proceeding in a pincer movement to join up with the northern invasion forces, and my General wanted to establish how far they had got. I volunteered to drive south and try and make contact. Intelligence briefed me to go first to Lyons, and my General wrote out my Movement Order accordingly.

As I approached the town, I was warned it was still in enemy hands, so I back-tracked to Paris from where I telephoned my General to tell him everything I had been able to find out. He told me to try again later, so I drove to Le Bourget to bum a ride to London.

September 23rd

My contact in the communications flight was a non-ops prick, I soon found out, and asked to see my Movement Orders. I said that I'd go fetch them, and departed for the nearest bistro where over two glasses of pernod, I changed Lyons to London, an inept job of forgery, I must admit, and when I presented it to him, he knew it was, and told me so. He could pull rank.

Not to be frustrated, I then told him that I was authorised to take these liberties with my orders, whereupon he wrote out an affidavit to this effect and made me sign it. As I climbed aboard the Anson, he grinned maliciously and said he would present the affidavit to the Provost Marshal. Under my breath, I told him to go fuck himself.

September 24th

Party in London lived up to expectations. Met a lot of chums at Shepherds and we took it from there all over town. I'd soon forgotten about what I'd signed.

September 26th

At Croydon, met up with chum Bob Constable-Roberts who asked me if I'd like to join his unit in Transport Command if I had a view to a post-war career in civil aviation. I said I had, and would get in touch with him. Caught the communications plane back to Le Bourget. The Communications friend asked if I had enjoyed myself, still grinning maliciously. I said I had.

September 28th

Told my General of my decision when I got back from Lyons, now taken over by the Americans. He said he'd miss me, but wouldn't stand in my way. Thought it a good idea. I didn't mention his Movement Order that I'd forged.

October 10th

The 70th Fighter Wing had moved to Aachen. Everyone in a bit of a flap about the appearance of Winston on account of security, except the good man himself who when confronted with a 'dragon tooth' fortification, unzipped himself and peed on it. I recollect that he was wearing his Air Commodore's uniform beneath his siren suit, and I basked in his reflected glory.

We heard the noise of some Daimler Benz motors overhead, but he didn't even bother to look skywards, as we all did, with a certain amount of apprehension.

October 20th

Bade a rather sad farewell to my General, drove my Auto Union Horche back to Laon, mounted up my Spitfire and high-tailed to Croydon, with my kit stowed in a parachute bag lodged behind my seat. Bob Constable-Roberts was pleased to see me, but somewhat apprehensive about the custody of my liberated aircraft.

I told him I'd dump it back at Supermarines, its place of birth, and that seemed to satisfy him, but a very sad day for me, however. Now, with the impending finish to my five years of warfare, I felt it time to look forward to a civilian future, which I had not dared to before, and civil aviation had become my goal.

October 24th

Letter to my father. RAF Croydon.

'I am just off to Paris to embark upon a new line of business.

Running an internal European airline for the wing. I enclose the letter from Gray Dawes, and after a considerable amount of thought, I feel it would be as well to maintain this string to my bow.

'The P and O syndicate are now more than interested in civil aviation, and all being well, by the time this war is over, I shall have amassed a considerable amount of knowledge about running an airline. It is the thing I am most interested in, or anything to do with civil aviation, and with my background of Vickers and family entrée into shipping lines, I have the opportunity to make it my life's work, which God willing, I now intend to do.

'I am well in with BOAC at the moment but a Government controlled outfit rather frightens me. I feel that shipping companies are bound to get into civil aviation, as they are now left with a lot of capital, but no ships, and I understand from a Parliamentary adviser friend to the Government that BOAC may not be the exclusive instrument, in which case independents will stand some sort of chance.'

CHAPTER TWELVE

Twin Engines

November 1944

Paris. My endeavours to start an airline between Le Bourget and Croydon proved a complete disaster. Not on account of my mismanagement, I may say, but on the ageing Anson's endemic fault. A structural weakness in the tail wheel assembly which was prone to collapse when running over rough ground, and now difficult to replace. One after the other, my fleet of aircraft went u/s to the point where my airline became inoperable, and I returned to Croydon.

My next assignment was to establish a staging post at Bordeaux, and I flew down as second pilot of a DC3, carrying a crew of mechanics and Tony Pulitzer (of the prize family), our unit Adjutant. Pulitzer had only one working eye, and had experienced considerable opposition to his enlisting in the Royal Air Force on account of this, and the fact that he was a middle-aged American. However, he overcame these prejudices by communicating directly with his friend Lord Beaverbrook, Minister of Aircraft Production, who arranged an honorary pilot officer's rank. Pilot Officer Pulitzer was a great Anglophile and had maintained, previously to the war a residence in London, a very good cellar and a chauffeur-driven Rolls, and as soon as he had completed his operational tour in Coastal Command he endeavoured to re-establish his customary way of living. However, again he ran into prejudice, this time in the form of petrol rationing. His entitlement as a pilot officer in relation to the consumption of his Rolls just didn't reconcile, so again he approached the Minister with a scheme which succeeded in overcoming this. He bought a castle in Scotland, which he endowed and maintained as a rehabilitation centre for air crews, and which he was entitled, as the benefactor, to visit once a month, for which the necessary petrol coupons were gratefully supplied. He also moved the most valuable of his wines there to escape the bombs, and apart from an occasional visit to his cellar his petrol ration subscribed to the transportation of guys and dolls in and around the pleasure spots of London and the home counties. The airfield at Bordeaux was in the hands of the FFI who made us welcome, and asked what our mission was. We filled them in on our intended staging post, that we would need accommodation for our maintenance crews and staff and as much transport as they could get their hands on.

We had brought with us a consignment of petrol in two gallon cans. They said they'd take care of the rest, as they had taken care of any Germans who had been caught or left behind, patting their assortment of weaponry from Luger pistols to butchers' knives, fastened to their belts. We filled their leader's car up with petrol, and he drove us in to town where we were accommodated in the best hotel. We'd left two of our roughest looking boys on board with Tommy guns.

Over dinner, served with champagne, their Captain, an evil-looking hombre, sparked when he heard Tony's second name was Pulitzer, and Tony had produced a wad of travellers cheques intimating that there was plenty more where they came from, for good service rendered.

When we were driven to the airfield in the morning by evil face, there were rows of cars lined up on the perimeter track. We tanked up six of them, left the same number of drivers, and Tony handed over a couple of thousand dollars worth of travellers cheques which seemed to satisfy. Then, saying *au revoir*, until the next meeting, while Pulitzer patted his pocket, we climbed aboard the DC3 leaving our six drivers behind, in what we prayed were Allied hands.

December 15th

Returned to our Croydon HQ with Tony Pulitzer, then up to London to visit his banker for the acquisition of more Travellers Cheques. Evening ended up at the Milroy Club with Glenn Miller whom Tony knew. Glenn told us he was flying to Paris on the morrow for the opening performance of his band, and insisted that we join him for the celebration. I'd checked with the Met Office who had told me that the weather was going to prove a very sticky situation, and I warned Glenn's pilot that I wouldn't attempt it, but he insisted that he would. I thought of the similar warning I had given Chris Leroux in similar circumstances, a few months previously, and Tony and I decided that we would skip this one.

When we returned to Paris, two days later, we heard that Tony's friend had never made it.

January 1945

Our 'liberated' cars had arrived safely at Le Bourget which was our French HQ, and we became the envy of the Parisiens as we drove around in style, the Ritz Bar as our main watering hole.

February 1945

We set up further staging posts in Europe in similar manner, with Tony Pulitzer's inexhaustible travellers cheques paving our way.

February 10th

Flew in to Rome with Bob Constable-Roberts and Tony Pulitzer. Romans all olive oil, obsequious and protesting their personal innocence. All the fault of Benito Mussolini the rabble had just hanged upside down. Made me sick.

Met up with Bill Hearst in the Excelsior Bar, and after a magnum of champagne had been consumed, he and Tony decided to call on the Vatican, but I declined. Wandered around looking at the lovely city which had remained untouched by warfare.

Rendezvoused, as arranged, six o'clock, Excelsior Bar with my friends who had had an audience with the Pope. Rather regretted I hadn't accompanied them. Bill said he hadn't realised he should have held some religious token to be blessed by the Pontiff until he had seen Pulitzer's action, but found some poker dice in a pocket which got the Papal blessing, in a closed hand.

He was all for starting up a game, on the bar counter, there and then.

February 14th

Flew in to Athens via Bari, leaving Bill losing heavily with his poker dice blessed by the Pope. As we came into the airfield circuit, saw Very lights being aimed in our direction, then spotted a large transport plane American marked and escorted by six P.51s. We got the message, and held off, until the cavalcade had landed, with scores of cars to greet them. On landing we discovered Churchill had arrived from Yalta.

Got a lift into town, and rooms at the best hotel. Found Randolph propping up the bar, or rather, the bar propping up Randolph who was holding forth, as usual. We moved down to the far end, so as not to get involved.

February 15th
Mission completed, we set off back to England, and landed at Croydon just before dark.

March 2nd
The Provost Marshals were beginning to bother me about my General's forged Movement Order, and what with that added to some questions about an unclaimed Spitfire with A.C.B. markings, Bob Constable-Roberts suggested it might be propitious to settle in Europe, and had me posted to 19 Staging Post we had set up in Brussels.

My appointment was second-in-command, and we had an establishment of jeeps, trucks and an Anson which no one would fly, except me, since it had been deemed as unsafe on account of some reputed structural weakness in its *empennage*. I had decided to risk it.

My first responsibility was to acquire officer's accommodation in the town, and fill this with booze. My powers of requisition were limited, as we were the guests of an ally, so I had to settle for a whorehouse which had been a favourite haunt of the Wehrmacht, I was given to understand. Reluctantly, I evicted *Madame and les girls*, and moved in my officers.

I was able to commute regularly to London, and upon one such occasion bumped into my friend Jack Dunfee, agent and impresario, in Les Ambassadeurs. Jack bet me he'd see me in Brussels the following week, and knowing my propensity for pretty girls, added that he would then introduce me to the prettiest I'd ever seen.

I didn't pay much attention at the time, as I reckoned that he was about the biggest show biz bull-shitter, ever.

March 6th
Got a call from Flying Control to say that a civilian gentleman had just landed from a Dakota and was asking for me, so I sped from my dispersal hut, around the airfield, to find Jack, enveloped in a vast fur coat and standing on the tarmac.

While I whizzed him to his hotel in my jeep, he told me that he was with a company of ENSA and was putting on a road show of Gaslight with Stewart Granger and Deborah Kerr, whom he'd like me to meet. A date was made for that evening, and Jack said that we were dining with our mutual friend, Aubrey Baring. When I arrived at Aubrey's headquarters, a magnificent town house requisitioned from a leading abortionist, Jack was already there, grinning from ear to ear and introduced me to Deborah Kerr. Formalities over, we got down to the cocktails and small talk whilst I appraised this plump and lovely red-headed actress.

Before the end of play I managed to get Deborah to myself and suggested that since I had transport at my disposal I could show her the sights of Brussels the following day. We tore around Brussels in my jeep, and I religiously attended two performances of the play, and on the last night of their stay I asked Deborah for a date which was accepted.

The way she looked when she came to meet me in the hotel lobby, I will always remember. Strawberry complexion, a shy warm smile and a little plumpness accentuated by the Khaki uniform she wore. We wined and dined and talked and danced, and before I dropped her back at the hotel I tried to kiss her unsuccessfully. The next morning, as arranged, I drove her to the airport to catch her plane, and I asked if I might call her when I was next in London. She scribbled her number and address, and said she would look forward to it.

10th April 1945- Belgium. Letter to my parents.

'Things are looking pretty bright out here, and the war seems to be over bar the shouting. I am still awaiting to liberate another capital before I pack up and come home. I heard that Ronnie Monteith, Cynthia's brother had been killed, but have not been able to verify it yet. Pretty bad luck to fall at the last fence like that. The Huns have absolutely 'had it' and have started snivelling. The chaos and destruction is too incredible to imagine.

'I met an absolute whizz-kid of a girl out here the other day. I am afraid it's another actress, but, oh boy, what a peach. Maybe, I'll grow up one day!'

April 25th

My unit was ordered up to Celle, a pre-war established Luftwaffe airfield just north of Hanover. I flew myself up in our old Anson and first circled over the skeletal city looking down at what appeared like a ghost town. On approaching Celle I again wide circled the environment at about a thousand feet and became suddenly aware of a nauseating odour infiltrating the aircraft cabin, and beneath me saw a wired enclosure of rows of wooden huts, some concrete block houses and a vast rectangular pit, besides swarming inmates.

I landed at the airfield, taxied over to the Control Tower, and switched off. Soon, a jeep appeared to pick me up and ferry me to the officers' mess where I was greeted by Johnnie Johnson who was commanding the wing of dispersed Spitfires I had observed. Having asked me what I was up to, which I told him, he gave me a guided tour of centrally heated magnificence including lofty reception rooms, one with a minstrel's gallery, a large swimming pool and a cinema, and finally downstairs a spacious beer-cellar covered with murals depicting the history of the Luftwaffe in all its glory.

Over our first pint, he told me that what I had smelt and seen was Belsen concentration camp, and that, no doubt, my first task would be to help in liberating it with our transport aircraft, and that, in fact, he had a signal for me to contact my Group HQ in this respect, and thereafter, the officer commanding the camp, one Brigadier General Sepal.

After a few more beers and a gobbled lunch, I did both things, to be told that a jeep would be shortly coming to transport me the fourteen miles to Belsen.

As we approached the camp, the nauseating smell I had first experienced at a thousand feet greeted us with its overpowering effluvium and I wrapped my silk scarf around nose and mouth.

We pulled up in front of a Guard House at the entrance of a vast enclosure surrounded by a barbed wire fence at which clamoured and clutched the skeletal forms of its inmates. Smoke from burning flesh rose languidly skywards, and bulldozers were shovelling dead bodies into the giant burial pit. A Dante's inferno.

The first thing I saw when I entered the Guard Room was the senior British officer who had summoned me looking almost as pale and gaunt as the prisoners, and having introduced myself, he wearily pushed a form towards me over the desk at which he was sitting, and told me to sign it. Then an orderly approached and sprayed me all over, up trouser legs and sleeves, with white disinfectant powder. Through an open door to a room behind I saw a row of inanimate bodies which the General told me were those of the prison guards who had been knocked senseless by his Commandos before he could stop them. He then ordered me to see it all, and remember for ever afterwards.

As I made my way through the death camp, I encountered men, women and children diseased and emaciated beyond description.

Dead and dying strewn everywhere, some clothed in rags, some naked. Scarecrows crawling through their own defecation in an attempt to hold the hands of their liberator which they recognised me as, through their tears of relief, and I had to back away for fear of contamination.

I saw a dead mother and child, half born. Another child who had been thrown in a refuse barrel outside the kitchen complex; it had come to solicit food, I was told. I looked down into the vast and stinking excavation which served as a communal grave, and into which putrefying bodies were being bulldozed and dragged by ghoulish burial squads from the ranks of their torturers. I entered the huts with their stacked-up bunks, their rotting incumbents dripping one upon the other. I looked in gas chambers and by-passed ovens fuelled with the dead and belching abhorrent smoke.

I threw up twice before I had seen it all, and returned to the Guard House to get my orders from the demented Commander to report what I had seen and return with medical volunteer help from England. My Wing flew in a medical group soon after. He told me where I could locate the 'Beast of Belsen' as he had become known, at an army campsite on the road to Cell, and that I should go see him, as well. He'd had him removed before the prisoners or his Commandos could get a chance to kill him. Also, Irma Grese, his notorious confederate who made her lampshades out of human skin, and now imprisoned in Cell jail.

I found Kramer in a large tent, chained by his legs to the pole, and guarded by a sentry, diminutive in comparison, whose fixed bayonet kept off his would-be assailants. He grovelled, pleading that he was only carrying out the orders of his superiors.

In May, we moved up through the smouldering ruins of Hanover and Hamburg in support of the advancing Allies, fetching and carrying in unarmed transport planes and setting up our Staging Posts.

I flew into Kiel to test the serviceability of the airfield, and was summoned by the Admiral of the British fleet of occupation to report to him on his flagship. After several pink gins, he told me my orders were to fly a German civilian, with naval escort, to London, first light in the morning. Top priority, and no questions to be asked.

I was intrigued by the little, innocent and professorial looking captive when he arrived with his escorts the following morning with a pile of cases. I reckoned that the Anson wouldn't get airborne with all our weight and said that one of his escorts would have to stay at sea. Bit of an argument, but as aircraft skipper, I won it.

Landed at Croydon, our captive approached me, and asked me if I knew who he was. When I answered that I didn't, he said with some pride, 'I am Professor Walter. President of Walter Werke. I make the engine for V1. Not good enough, I tell Hitler. But V2 I also make, was good, Ja? You had big trouble, Ja?'

When I'd agreed, and asked him what he was up to next, he replied tapping his briefcase, 'I read paper to the Royal College of Science on rocket fuel propulsion. Then, I go to America.' It didn't seem to occur to him the death and destruction that his devilish inventions had perpetrated, and that he was now a prisoner.

CHAPTER THIRTEEN

Safe Landing

Dramatically, but not unexpectedly, the German war came to an end, and I flew back to London to celebrate with Deborah. We paraded with the crowds in Piccadilly Circus, laughing and cheering, then repaired to her flat to drink a bottle of champagne and confirm our love.

No one knew when demobilisation would start, and within a few days Deborah went off to Ireland on a film location. When I confided to Janie that, for the first time in my life I wanted to get married, she just snorted, 'It's just another one of your girls, Bolshie, and only because the war's over.'

Stewart Granger warned me 'Never marry an actress, old boy. Their careers come before everything, and Deborah's no exception.'

Lonely without her, a few nights later I wandered into the 400 Club and ran into Whitney Straight, previously distinguished fighter pilot, now head of Transport Command. He was an American millionaire of whom it was rumoured a million dollar payola had been made, to effect his escape after being shot down in France at the beginning of the war.

'Bolshie,' he greeted me. 'You're just the chap I'm looking for, come and sit down.'

As he poured me a glass of champagne, he continued, 'There's a strong feeling among the Americans that we're not interested in their war against Japan, and I'm looking for volunteers to help out in the Pacific.'

'Then you're looking at the wrong man,' I replied. 'I'm going to get married and settle down.'

Whitney choked over his glass. 'You must be kidding,' he said. Two bottles later, I had agreed to go to the Pacific.

To this day, I don't know whether this was on account of Whitney's champagne going to my head, uncertainty about a state of matrimony, which I'd never previously contemplated, my incurable maverick nature or the relentless pursuit of the Provost Marshals who were now breathing down my neck. So far, I had been able to stall them by re-iterating my original false statement that I was authorised to alter the Movement Orders of my General, and that I had written him to confirm this.

What, in fact, I had written was a confession of what I had done, my present predicament in consequence, and would he kindly confirm my statement, otherwise I'd face court martial. So far, I had received no answer. However, looking back in all honesty I feel that my decision was predicated upon a commitment I had made to myself to partake in the war to its bitter end for a very personal reason.

July 1945

When I told my parents of my decision, they did not try to talk me out of it. How could they? Their other beloved son was at war in Burma as Medical Officer to a battalion of the Seaforth Highlanders. His medical unit had been one of the first to land and retrieve the wounded from the British beachhead in Normandy. Sister Patricia had helped break the German codes at Bletchley Park. My father and uncle had promoted the fund-raising in Bengal to buy the Spitfires for my old squadron which had become named 92, East India Squadron.

On the eve of my departure, I ran into David Niven in the Savoy Hotel and confided my situation, as one Old Stoic to another. He helped me write out my telegram of proposal to Deborah in Ireland, based on our love, and an offer of a civilian job as test pilot and sales representative of Vickers Armstrong when I returned to peace.

Thereafter, I packed my tin trunk and caught my train for my last staging post. My ship sailed before there was time to get the answer to my proposal.

On July 3rd the SS *Mauritania* sailed out of Liverpool harbour loaded to its plimsoll line with repatriating Allied prisoners of the European war, and a number of others like myself destined to carry on the fight against the Japanese in the Pacific.

When it reached its first port of call, Panama, the American Red Cross greeted us with brass bands, hot dogs and iced Cokes, only to be spurned with antagonism and a chorus of 'go home Yanks' from the Australians. A conflict with the Military Police ensued, and about a hundred POWs failed to rejoin the ship when it sailed. Similar confrontations took place in Honolulu and, this time, about three hundred were left behind in custody.

When we docked in New Zealand, we retrieved most of them

who had been flown there, by courtesy of the United States Air Force. Even aboard there had been fighting between Yank and Kiwi on account of coloured Maori troops being granted equal status rights by their white brethren.

What irony. What a gross finale to a war for freedom, I thought.

On August 5th, while still at sea, we heard rumours of an atom bomb being dropped on Japan…its horrific consequences, and momentarily my thoughts flashed back to the experiments in which I had participated in a Nevada desert.

On August 8th the SS *Mauritania* docked in Sydney harbour, and after a night of celebration on the town, I made my way to Melbourne, to report in at the Head Quarters of South East Asia Command, as my Movement Order had directed me. There awaited me two letters. One from Deborah, accepting my proposal of marriage. The other from an APO in Germany, Eagle embossed. I read:

> To whom it may concern. Squadron Leader A.C. Bartley, while attached to my Command, was authorised to change any Movement Order issued to him by me, and at his sole discretion.

It was signed, Brigadier General Macaulay. 70th Fighter Wing. 9th USAAF, and beneath, the P.S. 'Best of luck, kid.'

I had an interview with the Commanding Officer who told me my posting was to the Palau Islands in the Pacific which were occupied by the American Marines. My duties, to establish a Staging Post for Transport Command's route between Sydney and Hong Kong which was shortly going into operation. He also told me that the Provost Marshals were on my tail concerning an alleged forged Movement Order. I handed him my General's letter, and after he had read it, winked and told me to be on my way.

On August 17th I was flown in a Dakota to Townsville in the north east of the country, then on through New Guinea, Biak, until reaching my final destination Palau Island four days later. A military cemetery testified to the extent of the Marines' battle to recapture it. The heat was terrific, the white sand blinding, and the island 'dry'.

Letter to my family: Palau Island. S.W. Pacific. July 30th, 1945.

I have been away exactly two months, and not a word from anyone except Deborah. She seems to be the only person who cares whether the mosquitoes or the land crabs get me first.

I would appreciate a line to let me know how you all are.

Meanwhile, I am rotting on a desert island 7 degrees north of the Equator. My companions are American Marines and Japs. I came up through New Guinea and the Admiral Islands, and don't envy the unfortunate people who operate there.

I am going to marry Deborah, if she still loves me, when or if I return from the Pacific, and accept the Vickers offer to join them.

The US Marine Corps had it far worse than I did since they could not escape its boundaries, whilst I could fly the routes between Australia and Hong Kong with Transport Command. I also joined them in some of their fighter sorties against neighbour islands still occupied by Japs, on ground strafing missions.

I picked up many and diverse displaced persons from missionaries to prisoners of war, for repatriation including an RAF aircraft mechanic who had been hiding out in the mountains of New Guinea, since his unit had been overrun by the Japanese. King's Regulations ruled that when a pilot was forced down in enemy territory, he would destroy his aircraft (we carried pistols to shoot the petrol tanks) before attempting escape, and that an aircraft mechanic, in retreat, should hang on to his tool kit at all costs. This one had, indeed, and when I disembarked him with other grateful refugees at my base in Sydney, he asked me if he could have a word with me in private.

Attached like a limpet to his only possession, his tool kit, I took him to my room and offered him a change of underwear. I said I was short of cash, but the RAF HQ would take care of this. Whereupon, he opened up his tool box and picked out a spanner which he asked me to take in gratitude. As I hesitated to accept his unusual gift, thinking him insane, he produced a pocket knife and scraped the tool, which disclosed it was made of solid gold. He confided that he had hidden out in the abandoned New Guinea gold mines, and with moulds, had spent his time converting his tool kit into a more profitable metal. I didn't accept his gift, and I didn't disclose his secret.

To my parents, Sept 1945, Palau Islands.

Thank you for your lovely letters which have just caught up. I have been chasing around China and the Philippines, and the postman has had a devil of a job finding me. I am glad you all love Deborah. Spiritually, if not physically, she is closer to me than anyone I've ever known. I love her so terribly much that it frightens me. We have seen so little of each other, and yet I feel I have known her all my life. We want to get married as soon as I get home. Vickers have offered me representation of all Vickers aviation throughout Asia. It is a wonderful opportunity and I have accepted. Deborah and I will have to scrape up our pennies to fly together whenever we can. I imagine that it will be the same sort of existence that you, and Daddy had, only easier because of the simplicity and swiftness of air travel, – 48 hours to Calcutta – Can you believe it. If I make a success of this first assignment I've been promised others nearer home.

At the beginning of October, I flew back to Australia with a couple of Marines I had smuggled off the island, and went to see the Air Officer Commanding SEAC requesting repatriation. He practically blew all his gold braid and asked why I should expect preferential treatment. In defence I mentioned Dunkirk, the Battle of Britain, North Africa, France, Germany, the land crabs on Pelilu and that I hadn't had a break in six years. When this didn't unbend him, I mentioned my fiancée, as a last resort, and our plans to get married, whereat his countenance dramatically changed. But how did I propose to get back to England? he enquired, to which I had already prepared my answer. A DC4 was returning to England for a major overhaul, and I had been asked to join the crew as supernumerary co-pilot.

'Well, see that you get married, and get back here within three weeks', he said. 'Leave granted.'

Palace Hotel, Perth, Western Australia, 7/11/45: to my mother.

By the time you get this letter I shall be in England, and probably married. I will have seen you anyway, and consequently there seems little point in writing.

However, there is a reason for it, and that is, that I wish to remember one day in the far future my feelings at this time. I wish to express my sentiments at this great turning point in my life so that I will be able to look back in years to come, and analyse what I am about to undertake, and why I am about to undertake it.

Tonight I sit in a second-rate hotel in Western Australia, the day after tomorrow Colombo. Then Karachi, Cairo, Malta and home. That is, if my plans are uninterrupted. Last night we had engine failure, and were obliged to circle for four hours to run off fuel before we dared land. That is typical of what my war life has been. Disappointments, dangers, and nervous exhaustion that I have tried to camouflage under a veneer of careless devil-may-care bravado, that was never really my true self. At heart, I think I am a child who just wants someone to love and care for me, and when I had got to know Deborah I knew she was that person. There has been little passion in our loving of such short duration but maybe that will grow, and it would seem almost absurd to even contemplate marriage, in normal circumstances, but life is not normal. I'm not normal. My total commitment to the war has utterly exhausted me, and maybe matrimony is my final capitulation as the result of this, in which case I'm being more utterly selfish, so God help me. Our two careers which we intend to pursue are in no way complementary and we are equally ambitious. Maybe Deborah even more than I, but I think I have found my girl who can face this scene. She has had a rough indoctrination to her young life, and beneath her outward gentleness, there lies a toughness which I admire. A clinging vine would inhibit me from what I have to do. We will have to live apart a great deal of our time, as you and Daddy did. So be it.

*

To summarise my war, I would say that I fought for what I believed was right to the limit of my capacity.

I am not quite sure whether I ran away from Africa or not, and I have often thought of those poor kids I saw on trial at the 'lack of moral fibre centre' on that bleak island, Sheppey, and wondered if this was my case. I intended to return to Ops, I tell myself, but was pre-empted by the Liberator crash which wounded me. Ironically named, and my salvation, as it worked out.

I think I only volunteered to go to the Pacific to ease a guilty conscience, and only sought an aircraft to shoot at Japs, and in turn, be shot at, to seek redemption. I will always think that the last time I fired my guns was an act of self-indulgence, for vindication of my performance in North Africa. I wonder how many of the other Few have experienced a trauma similar to mine but will never admit it?

Now I have got this confession off my chest, I will bury it in my past, but will always wonder about North Africa. Am I the hero that I've been made out to be?

We ran into more trouble off Java and had to force-land in the Cocos Islands. I was desperately wondering how to communicate this dilemma when a native told me of the transoceanic cable hook-up between England and Australia which was situated on a neighbouring atoll to which he volunteered to row me. There, I found a decaying edifice, occupied by two elderly gentlemen in soiled tropical shorts and shirts who were occupied in throwing darts at a Tarantula spider climbing up the wall. Having waited for a direct hit, I made my predicament known to them and they acquiesced to my sending a cable to Deborah to tell her that our wedding date might have to be postponed.

In Ceylon, we ran into monsoons which delayed us another day, but from then on it was comparatively plain sailing, and we touched down at Hendon on the fifth day after leaving Sydney. I regarded myself as fortunate, considering that the aircraft was falling to pieces, and the crew had been playing poker most of the flight.

When Lord Beaverbrook heard from Janie that I was back, he summoned Deborah and me to Cherkley. Our taxi driver was drunk, so I took over the wheel. When I invited the Beaver to come to our wedding, he replied that he seldom even went to his children's.

After a wild stag party thrown by Sailor Malan and attended by my ushers Robert Stanford-Tuck, Jamie Rankin and 'Laddie' Lucas, amongst some other survivors of the Few, the following morning I received a hand-delivered note from Lord Beaverbrook which ended with, 'My love and admiration for the accomplishments of you both'. Attached to it was a wedding present cheque for £200.

Deborah and I were married on November 28th at St George's Church in Hanover Square, and the last person up the aisle before the ceremony started was the Beaver who thrust himself down between daughter Janie and Stuffy Dowding, disregarding any directions from the ushers.

At our wedding reception at Claridges there was an amalgam of film folk including Sir Alexander Korda, fighter pilots and family. Air Chief Marshal Lord Dowding, now become spiritualist, got my father in a corner and asked him whether he could feel, as he could, the additional presence of my dead comrades, and my father replied that he was far more concerned with my earthly commitment to return to South East Asia.

Wedding Day

'Don't you worry about that, Sir Charles,' the prematurely deposed Commander in Chief of Fighter Command answered, 'I still have some influence in the Royal Air Force', which he proved on my honeymoon when I got notification from the Air Ministry that I had been repatriated to the United Kingdom.

When Deborah and I left the reception, we discovered that our car had a flat battery. We were pushed to a start from the portals of Claridges on our way to our honeymoon by a bunch of cheering fighter pilots, whose combined air victories well exceeded one hundred.

Four years later, in the bar at the Royal Air Force Club, I accepted a drink from another Air Chief Marshal.

'Bartley,' he said. 'That name rings a bell. God-dammit, Bartley. I remember, now. I granted you three weeks' leave to get married, and orders to return to my South East Asia Command. What the hell ever happened to you?'

'I guess I must have just lost my way, Sir,' I apologised. 'May I buy you a drink?'

'About time,' grumbled the Air Chief Marshal.

Index